URGENT LONGINGS:
REFLECTIONS ON THE EXPERIENCE
OF INFATUATION, HUMAN INTIMACY,
AND CONTEMPLATIVE LOVE

URGENT LONGINGS
REFLECTIONS ON THE EXPERIENCE OF INFATUATION, HUMAN INTIMACY, AND CONTEMPLATIVE LOVE

THOMAS J. TYRRELL, Ph.D.

AFFIRMATION BOOKS
WHITINSVILLE, MASSACHUSETTS

Published with ecclesiastical permission

First Edition
Fourth Printing
© 1980 by Thomas J. Tyrrell

Library of Congress Cataologing in Publication Data

Tyrrell, Thomas J.   1938-
  Urgent longings.
    1. Love.   2. Sex (Psychology)   3. Intimacy (Psychology)
4. Spiritual life.   I. Title.
BF575.L8T96   155.4   80-13813

ISBN 0-89571-009-9

Printed by
Mercantile Printing Company, Worcester, Massachusetts
United States of America

Without the correction, the reflection, the support of other presences, being is not merely unsafe, it is a horror—for anyone but God. . . . It is in the lovely creatures God has made around us, in them giving us Himself, that, until we know Him, save us from the frenzy of aloneness. . . .

George MacDonald
The Last Farthing

With this quotation in mind, I dedicate this book

To Carol Tyrrell

An affectionate wife, a good friend, a loving and "lovely creature," a presence, a gift.

Affirmation Books is an important part of the ministry of the House of Affirmation, International Therapeutic Center for Clergy and Religious, founded by Sr. Anna Polcino, S.C.M.M., M.D. Income from the sale of Affirmation Books and tapes is used to provide care for priests and religious suffering from emotional unrest.

The House of Affirmation provides a threefold program of service, education, and research. Among its services are five residential therapeutic communities and two counseling centers in the United States and one residential center in England. All centers provide nonresidential counseling. The House sponsors a leadership conference each year during the first week of February and a month-long Institute of Applied Psychotheology during July. More than forty clinical staff members conduct workshops and symposiums throughout the year.

For further information, write the administrative offices in Boston, Massachusetts:

The House of Affirmation
9 Spring Street
Whitinsville, Massachusetts 01588

CONTENTS

FOREWORD

Pope John Paul II, speaking in New York City on October 3, 1979, stated: "Love demands effort and personal commitment to the will of God. It means discipline and sacrifice, but it also means joy and human fulfillment." Each of us can apply his words to ourselves in a special and unique way. The married person, the single person, and the celibate person are called by virtue of baptism to the life of growth in love. Growth necessarily means discipline, sacrifice, joy, and fulfillment. The title of this book, taken from the writings of St. John of the Cross, summarizes the human desire for growth that knows its ultimate satisfaction in God alone.

Ignorance about how to deal maturely with our feelings of love, their significance for our interior life, and how these feelings can grow in a healthy manner has caused a great deal of confusion in the contemporary Church and society. This book offers thought-provoking reflections on the beauty of love in the development of human and divine intimacy. It integrates developmental patterns of adult life and the dynamic features of religious growth. Yet it is primarily psychological rather than theological. It is written by a psychologist and psychotherapist not given over to the narcissism so often found in contemporary "pop psychology." The science in this book will challenge religious professionals and mental health professionals alike, not because of its complex matter, but because of the profound insights that are the result of Christian reflection and meditation.

The central lesson of the Incarnation is that grace and nature cooperate in the person. God took upon himself human nature, and, consequently, that nature has been elevated and affirmed to function as a channel of grace. Nature never initiates the activity of grace, but since God has himself implanted laws in nature, it is logical to suppose that he will follow the natural patterns operative in the human personality when he works through grace. Since Christ has dignified human nature, the aim of any natural growth process is transformed "so that we shall reach perfect personhood, that maturity which is proportioned to the complete growth of Christ" (Eph. 4:13).

I know the author of this book well. He writes delicately of the human journey of love. I have met other Christian psychotherapists who have written about this human journey, and I have observed a great disparity in their writing and their manner of living. These persons know how to write in order to win popularity that compensates for their own inadequacy, but they lack the fundamental integrity to live with the human journey that means sin, reconciliation, and ultimate freedom in the Holy Spirit. Dr. Tom Tyrrell lives the human journey about which he writes so well in this book. As husband, father, and friend, Tom models well for those of us with whom he shares this human journey.

I am so proud of this book. I know the hours of work that went into it while the author at the same time kept a full schedule of clients for psychotherapy at the House of Affirmation and never neglected his family life.

Affirmation Books is happy to invite you to reflect on the content of *Urgent Longings*. We promise you a reading experience that will challenge your thought and encourage your faith.

Thomas A. Kane, Ph.D., D.P.S.
Priest, Diocese of Worcester
Publisher, Affirmation Books
Whitinsville, Massachusetts

March 19, 1980
Feast of Joseph, husband of Mary

PREFACE

This book contains reflections on the experience of infatuation and the vital role it plays in fostering both human intimacy and intimacy with the Lord. These reflections are not intended to be comprehensive; they do no more than scratch the surface on the topic of intimacy. Yet their mission is to rescue the human experience of infatuation and restore it to its rightful place in human spiritual development.

Everywhere the experience of infatuation is dismissed by being relegated to the scrapbook or scrapheap of memory. People are either nostalgic, bitter, or sad, but rarely neutral, about infatuation. Occasionally, people express irritation at my effort to salvage its reputation. Some have asked with indignation: "You would let people become infatuated?" I have responded that infatuation is one of those mysteries of human psychological, spiritual development over which we can have little control. Infatuated persons are quite literally overtaken by the experience. Infatuation is an experience to which people are called.

However, what does one say to a director of novices who is faced with community pressure concerning the exclusivity of two young novices who are obviously in love and always seek to be alone? What does one say to a young professed religious or newly ordained priest who is in love with the spiritual director? In each case, other members of the community or residence are ashamed, embarrassed, and generally perplexed about what is happening and what to do about it.

More often than not, community or seminary authorities attempt to terminate relationships involving infatuation. But such efforts to stop infatuation have been the occasion of much spiritual and psychological damage. I have met young and middle-aged religious and priests whose affective lives, both interpersonal and spiritual, have been deepened and enriched by the experience of infatuation. Experience has taught me that more damage is done by trying to stop infatuation than could ever be done by merely letting it run its course. Certainly, infatuation should be guided by persons who understand the experience, both psychologically and spiritually. But in the absence of such persons, perhaps we should leave infatuated persons alone and pray!

I am not altogether sure how the experience of infatuation has acquired such a bad reputation, particularly as it relates to our spiritual growth and development. But I suspect that psychologists are somewhat responsible. We psychologists tend to focus exclusively on the urgency and fantasy that accompany infatuation and to consign the whole business to adolescence. We have aroused fears by focusing only on the genital or erotic dimension. In pointing out this limited focus, I do not mean to question the integrity of psychological reflection. I simply wish to invite my readers to question their assumptions about infatuation so as to meditate more affirmingly on the experience.

The etymology of the word *adolescence* offers us our first clue to the positive aspect of infatuation. The word contains the notion of kindling (ME. *kindlen*) and growing older (L. *ad* + *alescere*). Thus adolescence, a transitional and perhaps transformative episode in our development, is a time of passion (*kindlen*) foreshadowing the wisdom that generally accompanies growing older (*alescere*).

Psychology teaches us that it is during adolescence that we are first overtaken by the experience of being infatuated. But does it teach that we can make infatuation happen or that the transition from adolescence to adulthood ends the possibility of becoming infatuated? If we believe these latter theories, perhaps we should call to mind Gabriel Marcel's advice that "the love of creature for creature . . . is perhaps like a prenatal palpitation of faith."[1] Adolescent love is intense and passionate. Because the enthusiasm of adolescent lovers for each other affects those around them, we often regard the lovers' infatuation with impatience. But perhaps we should view their experience as a budding expression of faith, the fruit of which might be a wisdom that will guide their interpersonal lives.

Speaking both psychologically and spiritually, developmentally the experience of infatuation only begins in

---

1. Gabriel Marcel, *Creative Fidelity* (New York: Noonday Press, 1964), p. 137.

adolescence. Infatuation is an invitation to participate in loving intimacy, but we humans generally cannot respond to this invitation until middle age or beyond. Psychologists are correct in speaking of the erotic urgency and fantasy of infatuation. The experience engenders powerful feelings, feelings that overwhelm and thrust the person into the world of fantasy. Infatuated people are romantic dreamers who have trouble seeing the beloved with any clarity. They are indeed motivated by the romantic ideal of being in love with love!

Infatuated people, "fired with love's urgent longings,"[2] are called to an experience of being overcome by something and someone that is beyond their own power. But, as John Dunne reminds us, they are first called to human intimacy.[3] In their initial response, they get in the way of themselves, for their response to the call of both human love and Holy Love is generally clumsy and too full of themselves to be called a loving or an intimate encounter. Their sense of urgency makes infatuated people trip over themselves and fall on their faces. But infatuated people also feel a deep longing that transcends adolescent urgency. They feel a restlessness that apprehends the being-in-love-with-love that is the earmark of infatuation.

Infatuated people are engaged in a journey during which adolescence is only a pinprick on the map. St. John of the

---

2. St. John of the Cross, "The Dark Night," *Collected Works,* trans. Kieran Kavanaugh and Otilio Rodriguez (Washington, DC: Institute of Carmelite Studies Publications, 1973), p. 295. The poem appears in Appendix A.
3. John Dunne, *Reasons of the Heart* (New York: Macmillan, 1978).

Cross characterizes this spiritual adolescence as a being fired by the urgency of love, but he notes that the journey inevitably moves us toward being able to participate in fragile intimacy with Love Himself. Infatuated people burn (*kindlen*) with the excitement and enthusiasm of being called to their first rendezvous with love. But what of the transition, the transformation in wisdom, the growing older (*alescere*) inherent in the adolescent state?

Perhaps we can clarify the issue if we examine the word *infatuation* itself. Ironically, its heritage is full of a rich imagery that extends beyond metaphor, touching the vitality of the experience while at the same time revealing the wisdom, the growing older, implicated in the etymology of the word *adolescence.*

Infatuation, as a term, has its roots in the history of human experience. The root that comes down to us means "to make foolish" (L. *in* + *fatuus*). Desert travelers during the Roman Empire used the phrase *ignis fatuus,* or false light. An *ignis fatuus* was no mere invention of the imagination. Rather, it was an actual desert phenomenon.

An *ignis fatuus* was known to the nomadic tribes and pilgrims who crossed the desert in caravans guided by the only signposts that were reasonably dependable, the stars. These desert navigators would plot their way from oasis to oasis using their knowledge of the heavens. The fierce bone-chilling desert winds and the absence of reasonably fixed landmarks made desert travel a painful affair. Predatory animals and hostile people often roamed the desert. Danger, the inhospitable terrain, the everpresent threat of windstorm, the everchanging landscape, and the cold night air increased the longing for an oasis to provide relief from the pain of desert travel.

Often the desert pilgrims would observe what appeared to be the flickering light of a campfire. This beckoning light was such a strong inducement to depart from the chosen route that even seasoned travelers would have to discipline themselves to be guided only by their planned route and their knowledge of the stars. Those who gave in to the impulse to depart from their singlemindedness found that they were pursuing a destination whose location changed with every hillock and dune. The campfire would be genuine, but its actual location might be miles from where it made its appearance. Yet the travelers found their imaginations and their paths illumined by the light of an unseen campfire that promised relief.

Thus, although an *ignis fatuus* was a flame that gave light, it could provide no real relief to the desert pilgrims' urgent need, for it was a light that beckoned them to depart from the singlemindedness of their chosen path. In giving themselves over to the urge to find relief from their lonely voyage and have the intimate contact of other people, the impulsive travelers would find themselves lost. They would find their path illumined by the light of desire, not by the knowledge of lived experience. They would find themselves distracted from the singleminded path of informed knowing. Thus perhaps the term *ignis fatuus* is more accurately translated as a flame that gives light but not warmth.

In this story of the *ignis fatuus* lies the essential psychological and spiritual significance of the infatuation experience during which we feel an urgent longing for relief from the intense loneliness of our human journey. In a sense, we humans are all desert travelers. We yearn for that warm, accepting connection with others that we call intimacy. The promise of relief from loneliness fires us with enthusiasm for flames that give light but not warmth. Our enthusiasm belies the inevitable confusion that accompanies the loss of informed knowing. We would do well to remember this fact when we are confronted with clergy or religious of any age who report that they are "in love."

The experience of infatuation beckons us with a genuine light. But the wisdom of age teaches us that this light cannot offer us the warmth of real love, for our response to the invitation of infatuation is too much on the side of excitement and enthusiasm and too little on the side of that quiet, thoughtful, respectful presence St. John of the Cross would call contemplation.[4] Yet in the distraction and distortion of infatuation we desire the singlemindedness, quiet, peacefulness, and clarity that wisdom teaches are part of authentic, intimate, contemplative encounter with both the human other and Holy Other. We will learn in the following chapters that infatuation is a call to slow down, to dwell in the presence of someone whom we love. We will reflect on the problem of enthusiasm, love's urgency, but we will ultimately see that infatuation is a call to quiet appreciation of tender, gentle, simple things whose beauty is lost when we rush about the universe busily engaged in some project or another. We will discover that in the lover's gaze there is a call to contemplate the beauty, wonder, and mystery that is immanent in all human beings. We will learn that while infatuation heightens our self-concerned (egocentric) being, it also promotes a transformation to an other-concerned, other-centered mode of being. We will discuss how infatuation helps pro-

---

4. St. John of the Cross, *Collected Works,* pp. 577-649

mote growing older, the transformation whereby we become beings who are the authors of their own behavior but whose lives are guided by the loving hand of Providence.

The themes discussed in the following chapters include: the human journey; genital sex, affectivity, and intimacy; human love: the need that binds; loneliness and the transformed self; and the allowing self and intimate knowing. These themes are intended to chronicle the epic of human growth from the illusory intimacy of infatuation to that authentic intimacy of disinterested, informed love spiritual literature characterizes as contemplative presence. They are also intended to show the importance of the infatuation experience in curbing the egoism, or natural narcissism, of human love and in cultivating the growing older, the discipline, the wisdom, and the singlemindedness that can dispose us to Christian Love. I hope that by reflecting on these themes, persons responsible for spiritual guidance and spiritual formation will be able to guide others through this very human experience in order that their way of relating to the Holy will be able to flow from and be grounded in the human.

The reflections in this volume are essentially psychological in perspective. But they have also been shaped by a study group on formative spirituality to which Carol, my wife, and I have been privileged to belong. Consequently, if anything of originality appears in these chapters, it has been shaped by the Holy Spirit as he spoke through the perceptions, insights, and intentions of our group. Thus I am deeply indebted to Reverend Raymond Bertrand, S.J., Brother John Collins, C.F.X., Sister Mary Jeannette Robichaud, S.S.A., Sister Mary Rose Clarisse Gadoury,

S.S.A., Sister Mary Claire Allaire, S.S.A., Brother John Hamilton, C.F.X., Carol Tyrrell, and, finally, Sister Lauray Boucher, S.S.A., whose culinary artistry inspired us during our many hours of deliberation. In addition, I should like to express my thanks to Lynnette Perry for her editing and creative ideas and to the staff and residents of the House of Affirmation who offered their assistance in developing this book and the lectures on which it is based. I also thank Terry Murphy for her patience while typing and retyping the manuscript and Reverend Thomas A. Kane and Sister Anna Polcino for their encouragement and support.

I

THE HUMAN JOURNEY

Though nurtured like the sailing moon
In beauty's murderous brood,
She walked awhile and blushed awhile
And on my pathway stood
Until I thought her body bore
A heart of flesh and blood.

William Butler Yeats
First Love
from *A Man Young and Old*

When we speak of intimacy with each other and intimacy with God, we generally mean radically different things. But is the experience of authentic human intimacy so unrelated to the call to intimacy with the Father issued by our brother, Jesus Christ? Both invitations announce themselves in somewhat the same way: we feel that we are lured, beckoned, or chosen against our wishes; we resist being overcome; and, finally, we give ourselves over, we surrender to the beloved.

Unfortunately, when we speak of these experiences in the spiritual life, we tend to separate them from the human and wrap them in piety. Worse, we tend to split human intimacy from the Holy until we have a kind of spiritual neurosis. But here let us examine spiritual intimacy from the perspective of human interpersonal experience. I am not intending to suggest that the interpersonal route is the

23

only avenue to the Holy, but, like Thomas Merton, I would suggest that it is a most important route. Merton reminds us that we cannot attain sanctity by escaping from others.[1] His statement raises serious questions for us, questions that might be formulated in the following way: how can we witness to the Ethic of Love unless we are struggling to put Him into practice in our interpersonal lives? How can we really love each other unless we are reverent, accepting, nonjudgmental witnesses, unless we are "contemplative" in our expression of love? These troublesome questions are a logical counterpart to Merton's belief that human intimacy is an important route to travel on the way to sanctity.

How do we humans love each other? The romantic illusions of our culture would have us believe that we humans are ready, willing, and able to heed the call to intimacy with each other. Our secular literature, if not our television commercials, instructs that when love calls we go dashing off across the field into the awaiting arms of the beloved. Our spiritual literature, on the other hand, often seems pietistic and ethereal. But love rarely calls us the way we imagine it should. The disembodied, erotic, ethereal love of either profane or spiritual fantasy may have us go tripping freely among the daisies or floating among the clouds. But when we are touched by love on the plane of human existence, we undergo both blushing enthusiasm and considerable pain.

The spiritualized literature is correct; pain does make us wise, and the searing pain of first love makes an impression

1. Thomas Merton, *New Seeds of Contemplation* (Gethsemane, KY: New Directions Press, 1961), pp. 52ff.

to which we remain attached until well into middle age and beyond. All of us tend to be captivated by "beauty's murderous brood," and we are simultaneously touched by the blushing innocence of newly awakened love, a love that in the beginning always tyrannizes us by its delicacy and its erotic urgency. Neither our culture's literature nor our personal fantasy dwells on the moments of painful loneliness. Obviously, both sacred and profane writings need to be more integrated so that novices, seminarians, and middle-aged priests or religious can make sense out of that loneliness that makes them yearn for intimacy.

Later we will reflect on John Dunne's insight that the real wisdom of intimacy begins when we can allow ourselves to stop clinging to our painful loneliness. Now, however, let us consider that we grow wise to the way of intimacy not by wallowing in that delicious pain, but by disciplining ourselves to forget our adolescent, urgent longing for that all-consuming pain so easily reawakened when we reminisce about our first love, the love we, as infatuated people, secretly harbor as the only *real* intimacy we ever experienced.

When telling the story of spiritual intimacy from the perspective of human interpersonal life, we may begin with adolescence. For it is then that we are first fired with love's urgency, then that we first experience the delicious, searing pain that haunts us through middle age.

THE ADOLESCENT PATHWAY
TO BECOMING INTIMATE: FIRST LOVE

When we recall the experience of first love, which typically occurs between the ages of thirteen to twenty-five, we remember our affective sexual awakening. We awaken to the urgent longing of eros. We also awaken to loneliness as a painful yearning, experienced most sharply when the beloved is absent. In the absence of the beloved, we make an intuitive discovery about human sexuality. We discover we are separate yet oriented toward each other. When we are concerned for two persons who are "in love," perhaps we would do well to observe them when they are separated. For adolescent lovers are not just learning about genital feelings. They are learning about intimacy and loneliness, the warmth of closeness, and the pain of separation. When separated, the lovers act as if they are suffering the death of the loved one.

In adolescence, we are not just awaking to the genital aspect of human interpersonal life. We are awaking to eros, or, as C. S. Lewis would explain, to longing and to loneliness.[2] Eros is not merely a genital feeling, not just sexual excitement, but a call to be deeply, personally touched. It is a call to intimacy. It is a call to go beyond ourselves. We are called up and out of ourselves by another human being, and we are called to be ourselves, our deepest selves. Erotic awakening, our affective sexual awakening, is a call to empty ourselves, to give ourselves over to another human being. In adolescence, this call to adoration involves ecstasy and pain.

It is during our first experience of adolescent infatuation that we begin to hear the call to the commitment of mature love, that we are initiated into the intimate life of contemplation, of reverence for the simple, the tender, in our interpersonal lives. The urgent longings of adolescence

---

2. C. S. Lewis, *The Four Loves* (New York: Harcourt, Brace, Jovanovich, 1960).

awaken us to the charism of intimate love, but within the experience we are also called to awaken in wonder to the simple, the ordinary, the gentle, the tender. We are called to quiet reverence with another human being. Genital feelings get transformed from urgency to tenderness. For example, the desire to be relieved of one's own genital tension can become a desire to husband, in the archaic sense of cultivating the life of another, as a farmer tries to bring together the natural elements of water, sun, and earth so that a seedling might grow. Yet those who are captured by adolescent urgency are not able to so husband their own feelings. This function falls to those who are responsible for the adolescent's well-being.

In adolescence, this first "call to love" can be directed toward an important adult, peer, or member of the same or opposite sex. When the call is directed toward someone of our own sex, our western culture generally interprets the experience in a way that makes us either repress or deny our same-sex infatuation. But infatuation, in spite of its erotic dimension, is blind to gender. Yet it is profoundly sexual, seeking to affirm human eros, longing, and loneliness, in an attitude of reverence for others.

In any event, the presence of our loved ones evokes in us a feeling of being pulled toward them, of being literally called "up" and "out" of ourselves. Those whom we love evoke in us a feeling of awe. They seem to walk in mystery, a mystery that is often an unspoken command to follow, to imitate their every action, regardless of its significance. They seem to radiate magic; their touches, their smiles, any ingratiating gestures, real or imagined, serve to provoke in us ecstasy.

We develop a heightened awareness of the loved one's flaws and imperfections, but we are blind to their meaning. We ignore personal shortcomings and transform negative characteristics through a tolerance that is notable in its lack of wisdom or prudence. Our tolerance is complete, for our sense of uniqueness enables us to feel united to the beloved in a certain wonderment. Our involvement and loyalty are total; the beloved's wishes, needs, and desires prevail while ours recede into the background. We desire only to serve in willing obedience. Our primary concern in life is to be totally giving, totally open, and to express eternal love and faithfulness.

In the absence of the beloved, we feel utterly lost. Life intensifies, and the distractions of ordinary daily living intrude upon us. We experience ordinary life as pressure and dullness at the same time. We feel terribly bored and deliciously depressed. The pain is simultaneously unbearable and exquisite!

When infatuated, we feel elements of both holy and human intimacy. We feel a desire to reveal and offer the most intimate dimension of our being—ourselves. In adolescence, our physical self is developing; thus we feel a desire to promote the happiness and welfare of another through physical expression. We are truly other-centered (allocentric),[3] and in this attitude we experience an intense

3. This term combines the Greek *allon* and the English *centric,* meaning an attitude of being awesomely other-centered. I use this term in contrast to the rather selfish attitude of being ego-centered (egocentric). Moreover, when I speak of allocentricity, I mean to also refer to that attitude of respectful acceptance conveyed by the French phrase *apprisvoiser,* often translated as "taming," but I think more properly translated as "letting the thing (creature) be itself in all its wildness."

desire to empty ourselves through our bodies, through sight, sound, smell, taste, and, especially, through touch. Our giving seeks to promote the beloved; it is not a means to another end. It is an unconditional giving. We love others for the persons we imagine and feel them to be, not for how they behave or what they can do for us. Yet we harbor a deep fear that something is missing. This "something" is hard to define; it simply announces itself as tension or insecurity.

A hard reality is inherent in this first experience of love outside our family. For while adolescents experience moments of interpersonal reverence, they are too insecure in the world of mature love, love that calls for an awareness of life situation and the protection of commitment. This insecurity creates a tension that forces adolescents to seek the safe refuge of fantasy. In their fantasy, they can maintain the idealized image of the beloved and protect themselves from their anxious feelings. But in this imagined world the beloved becomes a love-object. The reality of who the beloved is in ordinary life gets manipulated by the adolescent imagination. In general, infatuated persons try to sculpt a new being, one that readily conforms to the values they are striving so hard to impress on themselves. This effort inevitably promotes tension. During adolescence, peers accept this tension in their relationship as part of the contract that binds them to each other, a contract sealed with outward signs such as the exchange of rings, photographs, or gifts.

Infatuated adolescent peers each feel the delight and pressure of being made into an idol. But, eventually, the pressure wears, for each has been asking the other to be God. As the experience runs its course, it becomes a burden. Gradually the imagined expectations begin to spill over into reality, where they are experienced as demand.

In adolescent infatuation, the romantic idealization of love—being in love with love—cannot get freely translated into the practical reality of everyday life because adolescents lack the experience to translate the ideal of love into love *of* and *for* another person. In the course of their relationship, the "lovers" often begin to experience frustration and anger because their loving gestures, gifts, and many acts of kindness are not returned. They feel themselves to be failures at love, and they are. They have failed to realize that their generosity has been fired by a romantic ideal of an intensity that no mortal could really hope to realize or adequately return. Adolescents feel no reverence, no quiet; they are not able simply to dwell in the presence of others whom they love freely and deeply. Adolescent urgency prohibits freedom. Even the love songs of adolescence clearly picture the other as the object of need, urgent need, and urgency prohibits husbanding.

In the end, the press of ordinary life intrudes on the "lovers." They begin to awaken to the realization that each has been the *object* of attention. Often this realization occurs to one, then to the other. The one who first leaves the dream provokes the urgency of the other. But once either "lover" embraces the reality of ordinary life, admitting that the expectations are beyond the other's reach, both "lovers" make a remarkable discovery. The feelings that drew them together and appeared to bind them so tightly lose their strength. The "lovers," who had come to believe that the bond between them would endure forever, now discover that their urgency has promoted only an illusion that their covenant of love is protected by a curtain of steel. In embracing reality, they realize that human relations, like seedlings, are delicate. But they also discover that the illusion of fantasy spins a bond that cannot tolerate the harsh touch of reality. As they embrace reality, the fragile web of the adolescent dream world is torn, and there is no return. No amount of clutching can restore the dream.

At this point the "lovers" feel exposed to those around them, their secret having been discovered by a disapproving community. Shame follows, for their exposed secret makes them feel the embarrassment of having sought a false security, one determined by urgent need, an invention of their imagination, created by a need to protect their newly emerging self, the self of genital feelings, a self that is not yet the tender self it will become. Once exposed, the "lovers" must now confront the fact that in truth they really could not accept the lived reality of the beloved. They must now accept that the idol had real human limits. In their shame, they find that they must also accept their own limits, limits that are generally brought to attention by the very persons who have been the object of their loyalty and love.

The now-broken contract announces that they are once more alone. But this being alone is full of shame, for they have discovered that they have tried to invent another being, one who could offer fulfillment. Infatuation by nature tries to promote the notion that our fundamental aloneness, given in the reality of human sexuality, can be overcome. Infatuation tries to promote an egocentric vision whereby we find total personal fulfillment and relief from our deepest loneliness by centering our lives on other human beings. Infatuation offers the false promise that relief from fundamental aloneness can be gotten in *this* life.

But the pain of separation genuinely awakens adolescents to the wisdom of mature love. As they undergo their shame, they are forced into semi-isolation. As they withdraw to an imposed but shallow solitude to lick the wounds of their broken-hearted pride, they begin to be honest with themselves. In the naive openness of adolescence, which started the infatuation in the first place, they begin to realize that they have been living in fantasy.

In their isolation, they begin to awaken to the governing principle of interpersonal love: human love, like all living beings, has its season. The urgency to be loved begins to be tempered by the wisdom that love is only authentic when it is offered and accepted in freedom. They thus awaken to a fundamental principle of interpersonal life: relationship cannot be forced. Fortified by this wisdom, infatuated persons seem to gain a new sense of direction and purpose. The heaviness, pain, and confusion disappear. In adolescence, this disappearance often seems to happen overnight, or at least until a new idol appears on the horizon. But in adulthood and middle age, the loss of the beloved, whether it be a person, place, or some other love-object, is often experienced long after any personal resolution is achieved. Later in life the pain of lost love burns more deeply as death becomes more and more an inescapable reality.

YOUNG ADULTHOOD: INTIMACY WITH LIFE FORM

Obviously, the adolescent experience described above is synthesized and necessarily repeated numerous times before anything that even modestly approaches liberation begins to occur. But at some time the person achieves a peace of sorts, as the sense of urgency diminishes.

In the next decade of life, the twenties and early-to-mid-thirties, the story of intimacy changes as the horizon of the infatuation experience expands. Although the experience still includes other persons, it now involves life form in a more explicit way. We find ourselves called by vocation, and it seems that the life form chooses us. We are more forcefully drawn toward clerical or religious life, toward marriage, or perhaps toward the single life. Age forces us to make a career choice. But the decision seems to become easy as we move toward a choice that seems to choose us. The choice is further facilitated by that special someone who seems to have achieved perfection in the life to which we are drawn. With that person's appearance on the scene, the choice solidifies and seems to be the only avenue that can provide personal fulfillment and happiness.

Ordinarily, we undergo moments of doubt and uncertainty when we may question the relative worth of our chosen life form. But at bottom we harbor the notion that in truth it has chosen us. This life that calls us seems to provide a certain hope, a hope that it is the place in which happiness and fulfillment will be found. We may take vows, and as we utter the magic words, we open the door to a new life, a life full of hope and the promise of fulfillment.

In this experience of being captured, of being set-upon by a life that was lying in wait, a new dream begins. Our adolescent urgency, the longing for a flesh and blood idol, is tempered by the wisdom of our previous pain. We are still yearning to find happiness and fulfillment, but our desire to find an understanding other who will touch our lives in a personal way takes a different turn. At this point the story of human intimacy changes as we find ourselves drawn to those who appear to have achieved a sense of expertise in the life we desire.

William Kraft notes that this period is critical to spiritual formation in clerical and religious life.[4] He believes that at this point in life this desire to be personally touched is a search for a deeper spiritual fulfillment than is possible through the unrealistic search of adolescent fantasy. The young adults are infatuated with being priests, sisters, brothers, etc., but they continue to seek the compassionate, nondemanding acceptance of others who will be loving witnesses to the persons the young adults are, with all of their flaws and imperfections. They insist that they be accepted for the persons they are, not for the persons others might imagine them to be. Often this insistence results in intense personal and interpersonal scrutiny. The conversations of these young adults often become extraordinarily intense and personal, laden as they are with the weight of remembered pain and the fear of an unknown future.

When these young adults find the compassionate, nondemanding acceptance of an understanding person, they are again moved by the enthusiasm of infatuation. Usually this understanding other embraces the young adults' vocation. The other would do well to remember that he embodies certain life ideals to which the infatuated person aspires. Even beyond seminary or novitiate, young

---

4. William Kraft, *Search for the Holy* (Philadelphia: Westminster Press, 1972); idem, *A Psychology of Nothingness* (Philadelphia: Westminster Press, 1974).

adults in their clumsy intensity realize that they have not yet mastered the ideals of their profession. Although this realization is not fully conscious, it nonetheless provokes anxiety. In their anxiety to achieve mastery, the young adults once more seek the security of fantasy. From their hungry imagination, they often embellish ideal persons, such as their first spiritual directors, seminary rectors, or novice masters, with personal characteristics that are slightly out of focus. Yet this time their fantasy is a bit more attuned to reality. The ego-ideal will generally have the good qualities they perceive, and they will generally allow themselves to see his personal limits.[5] But they will tend to compartmentalize the flaws, creating something of a tension for themselves and the ideal person. In some situations, such as novitiate, anxiety to do well may not let the boxed-up flaws be contained, and the young adult's will-to-perfection may create tensions that are sometimes quite destructive. However, if all goes well in this period of aspirancy or courtship of life form, understanding others will feel only a certain intensity while in the presence of infatuated persons. The others need not distance themselves unless they have failed to realize that they cannot live their own vocation to perfection.

The relationship will be sticky nevertheless, for the young clerics or religious are also infatuated persons, and they want more than anything to be intimate with their chosen ideals. They want to be touched in a personal way by this life that seems to have chosen them. Thus they need

---

5. When the adolescent experience is repressed or denied, or when more serious psychopathology is present, distortion will be considerable. In either case, psychological therapy is needed.

to be gently reminded that they are living "in the middle," that they are still living the adolescent fantasy of finding the perfect priest, brother, or sister after whom they can pattern their lives. They need to be reminded that they are nowhere near to being even modestly proficient at their chosen life in any lived way. They need to be reminded that although they may desire a certain life form and perhaps even possess the intellectual proficiency for it, that proficiency needs to be converted into practical reality. In being told the story of intimacy, they must come to realize that proficiency is aided by imitation and not by the mimicry of infatuation.

The idealized person, the object of the infatuation with life form, can help to foster an appreciation for the limits of the situation by not pretending to *be* the ideal. Too often the idealized person happens to be the one in authority, i.e., the religious superior. The daily contact occasioned by this office places the idealized person in an untenable position. The tension promoted by the infatuated person is coped with more easily if the idealized person gives in to the seduction of perfection, if he consciously, or even unconsciously, pretends to live the life form according to the image of perfection perceived by the infatuated person. However, in the long run, this manner of coping creates more problems than it solves.

The discipline that the infatuated person demands of the other is not always easy to accept, for it requires that the other encourage the infatuated person to be faithful to the position of being "in the middle." Being in transition is always a position of tension. The older person is called upon to witness for tension and anxiety. Obviously, it is much easier for that person to act as if he has all the answers and then to patronize the infatuated person with acts of condescending encouragement.

It is an irony at this stage of human development that the desire for understanding can promote hope for inner peace only to the extent that it witnesses to tension. If individuals are to promote intimacy with the chosen life form, if they are to foster any sense of understanding, they must so witness. Such witness will help infatuated persons to be faithful to the reality of their life situation at that moment in their history. It will encourage them to take up an awaiting stance whereby they can begin to be released from the urgent need to be perfectly proficient in their chosen way of life.

At this period in life, the witness of significant others promotes a sense of recollection whereby the wisdom acquired in adolescent solitude can reassert itself more fully. Patience fostered by significant people who understand the young adults' anxiety to do well will promote a willingness to accept incompleteness. Touched by loving, understanding acceptance, infatuated persons are able to live their anxious tension in more creative ways. The urgency to be at a point of espousal with their chosen life now becomes a desire to find their rightful place in the cosmic plan. The interior patience engendered by an understanding, accepting other (one who also accepts his own place as a person *on the way*) also allows infatuated persons to accept their fitness for their chosen life in a more realistic way.

ADULTHOOD: WHEN LOVE'S URGENCY DIMINISHES

In large measure, the period of young adulthood is critical in developing our ability to take up the con-

templative attitude, i.e., the attitude of quiet, nondemanding, reverent acceptance, the attitude that fosters intimacy.
In the period following adolescence, we generally become
committed. The awaiting stance, which flows from being
able to patiently curb our desire to achieve proficiency in
our chosen lives, enables us to move toward a certain
graceful expertise in the ability to be intimate. The story of
intimacy changes once more as we begin to become the
thing to which we aspired.

With adulthood, generally the period covering the thir-
ties and early forties, the desire for intimacy emerges in a
new and different way. At this point in interpersonal life,
love emerges as a less urgent, less romantic, and more practical expression. Kraft reminds us that the repetition of
everyday acts of kindness now takes on a new and deeper
significance.[6] Through these simple acts of being present
to others, we begin to realize the significance of dedication
and commitment. The desire for intense closeness with
others begins to loosen its claim.

Now the intense romantic yearning of adolescent infatuation is playing itself out. In its place comes the
realization that life is not fulfilled through intensity but
through simplicity. Human imperfection is now acceptable. The simple acts of daily living, held under such close
and intense scrutiny in young adulthood, are now able to
be celebrated. The skepticism and cynicism of the twenties
fade. The false and superficial no longer have to be com-
partmentalized; they can be viewed with a sense of humor.
Persons now find that they can have intimate moments
without being distracted by their previous need for inten-

---

6. Kraft, *Search for the Holy,* pp. 101-108.

sity. The urgent longing for a perfect life, one without negative feelings and experiences, diminishes, and the story of intimacy becomes a long but pleasant tale that promises a happy ending. With an attitude of graced acceptance, persons find that they can even appreciate feelings such as boredom, anxiety, or loneliness as messages that proclaim life and promote growth in being able to offer loving responses to others. At this point, life seems to be full of promise.

MID-LIFE: TRANSITION TO DEEP LONELINESS

Adulthood is a time of integration during which our identities as persons are formed. As we move into the middle years, usually between the mid-forties to mid-fifties, the experience of infatuation makes yet another attempt to seduce us with the promise that only human intimacy offers fulfillment. The story of intimacy seems to take a somewhat ominous turn. We find that there are times when we are too tired to listen to people. We have a difficult time focusing on the other's story; other-centeredness again shifts toward self-centeredness. In mid-life our identity as persons who are able to live the intimate life of contemplation is again thrown into doubt and confusion.

In the middle years, our bodies grow more tired. We experience our physical limits more sharply. In the matter of intimacy, this loss of vigor is initially experienced as a loss of our ability to be loving people. We know intellectually that we are both loved and capable of loving. But this knowledge seems to escape us on the feeling level, and we are too tired to care. At some level of consciousness, both lay people and celibates tell themselves that diminishing sexual potency and general slowing down are the culprits of the confusion. We are confused by our tired bodies. In our culture we are led to believe that sex is the vehicle of love and intimacy; so as the vehicle begins to slow down, we feel a loss in our ability to love.

Sexual feelings begin to be significant in their lack of urgency. Kraft notes that men at this stage begin to question their manhood. Women feel the onset of menopause and are confused by fluctuations between apathy and desire. Both experience depression as central to their lives.[7]

In the midst of this depression, confusion, and intense self-doubt, middle-aged persons begin to notice that the urgency of their interpersonal lives has diminished. They notice that their interpersonal encounters are characterized by an acceptance of the talents *and* the limits of others and that with this acceptance their personal lives take on a new richness, accented by wonder and surprise. While there are moments when fatigue makes them inattentive, they also remind themselves to curb their enthusiasm, to do a little less in order to be more fully attuned to others. With this insight, middle-aged persons find that they take less and less for granted and live within the context of incessant wonder and surprise, not of the spectacular, but of the simple. Their bodies, though tired, take on a more graceful way of moving, eating, sleeping, and playing; working, talking, and listening take on a new joy and pleasure. But these activities are less urgent and more simple. The story of human intimacy seems to be worth telling again.

Middle-aged persons find that they do not need to seek the company of others. Yet the presence of others is more enjoyable, for now they can laugh at their own shortcom-

---

7. Ibid., pp. 108-16.

ings, and their sincere self-acceptance invites others to do the same. The frantic search for intimate, loving, meaningful relationships becomes a quiet awaiting in the faith that they are loved and capable of loving.

Solitude now becomes a real possibility in life. Middle-aged persons can accept being alone, and in moments of solitude they feel a sense of deep reverence and respect for others, for reality, and for life. They experience little if any "narcissistic dialogue of the ego with itself."[8] Rather, they feel a pervasive sense of unity with self, others, life, and with the All That Is. Middle-aged persons view solitude as providing the opportunity to experience a sense of unity, not separation, and they bring this attitude into their interpersonal lives. Listening is less labored; they hear people in a way that enables others to feel understood and accepted. Even when they must correct, they speak in a way that respects the other's integrity, continuing to foster understanding and acceptance. The allocentric attitude is more and more incorporated into their everyday waking presence and becomes the dominant mode of relating to others. Middle-aged persons are more and more able to husband the feelings of others, especially those whose lives are dominated by urgency.

Now able to be alone, persons find that the adolescent desire to serve in willing obedience lessens in its intensity. This loss in intensity comes when the person achieves a sense of resignation to the harshness of life, but this awareness is not marked by the cynicism of youth. Rather, it is accented by a sense of reverence for life and for others. The knowledge that life is harsh liberates, detaches persons

8. Merton, p. 52.

from being too serious about clinging to life as the source of hope. They see their existence as a joke, and this insight provokes tears of laughter and relief. They thus become contemplative in the interpersonal life as they are more and more able to listen to others. They become liberated from the distraction of concealing the fact of their own imperfection.

The desire to serve now undergoes a curious change. Persons no longer feel the urgent need to serve those they love, for they realize that they can only be of service if they walk with them and appeal to them to be faithful, authentic witnesses to the limited reality of human love, care, and concern. They have discovered that they cannot force others to accept the promise held out by infatuation, that human love is perfection itself.

Infatuation loses its claim, for the middle-aged person begins to feel the finality of human life. With the realization that human life is limited and finite comes the realization that it cannot offer fulfillment, only moments of fleeting satisfaction. Intimacy loses its urgency, for the person perceives that it cannot be forced, that we can be intimate with others only by inviting them in loving hope. The raging fire of infatuation is now able to be displaced by the fragile spark of love. Intimacy is casual, comfortable, more relaxed, and less and less urgent.

With middle age comes personhood. When we resign ourselves to the fact that life is harsh, that it is limited, imperfect, and finite, we are able to be present to others selflessly and are free to be allocentric, to dwell reverently in loving acceptance of another who has the same right as we ourselves have to be imperfect. Acceptance of life's harshness loosens the urgency of infatuation, which is an urgency to perfection. With acceptance comes a deeper but satisfactory loneliness and a deeper solitude, one that promotes the possibility of more authentic intimacy with self, others, life, and the All That Is: God.

Having described the transformation of infatuation from the urgent longings of adolescence to the more casual, relaxed intimacy of mid-life, let us now turn our attention to a more detailed study of the experience. In the following chapters we will observe how the very nature of the infatuation experience is oriented toward developing the possibility of contemplative moments in our interpersonal lives.

II

AFFECTIVE SEXUALITY
AND INTIMACY

Truly you have formed my inmost being;
you knit me in my mother's womb.
I give you thanks that I am fearfully, wonderfully
made; wonderful are your works.

Psalm 139:14-18

It would be an understatement to say that people in religious or clerical life are scandalized when one of their colleagues falls in love. In the novitiate or seminary, the experience is barely accepted and is often ignored. Among middle-aged religious and clerics, it is generally not tolerated. Always it is important to distinguish infatuation from relationships that are mutually exploitive. This distinction cannot be made on the basis of age, however, especially in religious or clerical life in which people have too often been asked to postpone adolescence. Infatuation is not simply an adolescent phenomenon, but a phenomenon that begins in adolescence.

INFATUATION: AN INTERIOR AWAKENING

At any age, the infatuation experience signifies the awakening of a fundamental altruism shared by spiritually sensitive people: the desire to serve. At its onset, however,

45

the altruism is more ontological than existential. The first attempts to live it are awkward, clumsy, and infused with too much urgency. Bystanders are so caught up in this urgency that they often interpret the tenderness that infatuated people show toward each other as mere lust, erotic excitement, and search for genital pleasure. Infatuation is partly to blame, for the inherent mystery of the phenomenon makes the lovers enshroud themselves in secrecy. Those outside the intimate circle of love cannot apprehend that the attitude of infatuated people is the same as that of the psalmist when he sings: "I give you thanks that I am fearfully, wonderfully made; wonderful are your works" (Ps. 139:17-18).[1]

The tenderness, secrecy, other-centeredness (altruism), and incessant wonder of infatuated people are erotic, but not merely in the genital sense. The erotic feelings of infatuation simply are not synonymous with the lustful *treibe* or instinct referred to in psychoanalytic theory, for the erotic feelings of infatuation foreshadow more depth and richness. Sexual instinct is present, of course, and we would be both foolish and irresponsible to pretend that it is absent. But the urgent, erotic centering-on-the-other of infatuation goes beyond mere genital feelings. Unless sexually fixated, the erotic pull, posed by the charism of the other, goes beyond genital excitement. The erotic feelings that become visible during the early stages of infatuated

---

1. The ideas expressed in this chapter were first published in an article entitled "Intimacy, Sexuality, and Infatuation," in *Intimacy: Issues of Emotional Living in an Age of Stress for Clergy and Religious,* ed. Anna Polcino (Whitinsville, MA: Affirmation Books, 1978).

love are soon overshadowed by the emergence of the twin selves of simplicity and tenderness whose auras carry with them all the values that pertain to the interpersonal life of holiness. Tenderness and simplicity are sentiments far more powerful than lust; but in the early stages these sentiments are only implied. Those outside the lovers' circle observe only behavior that appears to be essentially erotic in the genital sense, and they often find such behavior threatening.

Why do we tend to flee from this eruption of beginning love? In intent, the erotic feelings of infatuation have little self (ego)-centeredness about them that could make them a real bother. Rather, infatuation is by its very nature *urgently* other-centered. The problem of infatuation lies not in its erotic dimension but in its urgency and the pressure that it creates. Indeed, the erotic dimension only foreshadows an altruism and charity that rescue infatuation from being a merely base human instinct for survival of the species, an identification that psychoanalysis mistakenly teaches.

Obviously, a host of problems accompanies the infatuation experience. The exclusivity of an infatuated couple in the seminary or the community arouses strong negative feelings, such as jealousy or resentment. Those outside the lovers' circle perceive the excessive demands each lover makes on the other. Outsiders see how clutching, maudlin, and sweet the lovers are; they see the pressure and lack of freedom inherent in the relationship.

Yet the infatuation call is authentic. It is a call to interpersonal care and to human intimacy. It is also a call for unconditional and respectful reverence for the totality of the other, the beloved, with no qualifications whatsoever.

It is a call to human, holy intimacy with another human being, and thus it is a call to chastity. Perhaps bystanders misinterpret the experience because care, love, and erotic urgency are all present and undifferentiated. They are fused together; consequently each is confused with the other. To focus only on tenderness and urgency and to dismiss even these as erotic in the genital sense is to miss the point.

Indeed, those who view the lovers from outside their intimate circle perceive acts of intense affection and immediately interpret those acts as merely genital. But the acts of affection have a deeper meaning not visible to the outside observer. It might be more helpful to think of infatuation as primarily an experience of being wholly and deeply touched by another person, not physically but personally. Although physical touching may occur, it is not really germane to the experience, for infatuated people seek to be known, accepted, and understood on the personal level.

Genital sexual urgency enters into the infatuation experience.[2] But the initiate is unable to differentiate this urging to sensual pleasure from the authentic holy intimacy that is the center of the experience. Novices in love are generally novices *at* love; they are simply too inexperienced to accommodate their lives to the horizons of meaning implied by their erotic feelings. They are confused at this point in their lives; so they misunderstand

---

2. By using the term eros, I mean to imply that special interrelatedness of sexual feelings and the state of "being in love" referred to by C. S. Lewis in *The Four Loves* (New York: Harcourt, Brace, Jovanovich, 1960), pp. 131-62. More will be said of eros later.

their feelings. They hear this first call to mature love as an invitation to be loving and be loved, but the urgency created in part by genital pressures makes this invitation a demand for love, a demand for care, a demand for intimacy. Infatuated persons say to their beloved: "You *ought* to let me love you; you *ought* to love me in return." They are unable to appreciate that love is the inevitable outcome, the fruit of relationship, cultivated by patience, care, and respect. They cannot yet appreciate that their demand for love can force the relationship to end before it has really begun.

Infatuation is simply unable to be thoughtful about love. Infatuated people insist on loving and on being loved. Their genital impulse displaces their thoughtfulness. Their sense of urgency and longing is too overwhelming to permit them to be reverent of others in a more simple, quiet way. They need the wise guidance of people who are thoughtful and patient, who have already integrated their own urgent longings.

Unfortunately, infatuated persons are typically surrounded by repressive people, people who have not attained the wisdom that enables them to be calm and accepting about eros, let alone about genital feelings. Consequently, infatuation gets reduced to and equated with genital sex, which C. S. Lewis asserts is only a component of eros. By so reducing the experience to the thing that promotes the urgency, those who seek to repress erotic feelings sabotage the experience, robbing it of its richness, aborting its growth. Genital feelings are like new growth: a too early pruning will destroy possibilities that at this stage are only implied.

REPRESSION AS A DENIAL OF INTIMACY

What is it that frightens us so that we feel we must repress infatuation? Why is it that we cannot dwell with erotic feelings without believing that they must be expressed in some sort of behavior? Why is it that some people must strive to purge themselves of affective sentiment, for themselves and others? In attempting to prune away genital feelings, do these people forget that we are incarnate spirit? The answer is a sad yes. Such people live as disincarnate beings, as if their bodies were a mere afterthought of creation. Their overriding taboo is "feeling," especially tenderness, care, or affection. They cannot experience, indeed, they cannot even acknowledge these responses, and since the self of affectivity (tenderness) is rather close to the self of genital sex, this response must be denied as well. Repressed persons do not have, or have lost, the interpersonal skill that Alan Watts calls the "art of feeling."[3] They are generally unable to express care, concern, or affection, and in those moments when they try to express these feelings, they do so without real warmth or tenderness. Watts characterizes such persons as "intellectual porcupines" who live out of their heads, putting thoughts before feelings, meeting others not with tenderness, but with a surface of spikes.[4]

These intellectual porcupines cannot cultivate the space and freedom so desperately needed by infatuated people. Such persons cannot husband the delicate growth that is emerging in the infatuated person, for they suffer from a

---

3. Alan Watts, *Nature, Man and Woman* (New York: Vintage Books, 1970), pp. 70-96.

4. Ibid., p. 81.

too severe pruning themselves. In an attempt to cut back their own urgent longings, they have cut them out altogether. Consequently, they have eliminated the possibility of the tenderness and the intimacy these longings can promote.

In therapy we often find that seriously repressed persons either have refused or are unable to be open and available to others on a personal level. Interpersonally, they suffocate the self of tenderness in themselves and in others. In thus refusing or being unable to express tender or gentle feelings of care or concern, they deny their affective sexual selves. In ordinary instances of everyday repression, persons do not pathologically deny their sexual feelings or identities. Yet they are uncomfortable with them and thus deny themselves and others the opportunity to express such feelings in a respectful, appropriate, and personal manner. William Kraft notes that such persons also rob themselves of the opportunity to be intimate with themselves in solitude; their moments of solitude soon regress into pietistic narcissism or, in more radical instances, degenerate into a schizoid existence.[5] At this point in their interpersonal lives, they become anonymous, for they have lost the possibility of being intimate. They are unable to cultivate either love of self or love of others. These are the people Thomas Merton addresses when he reminds us that solitude is not an escape from others but an opportunity for deeper intimacy.

In their avoidance of personal contact, repressed persons are, in fact, unchaste. They are unable to fulfill the

5. William Kraft, *The Search for the Holy* (Philadelphia: Westminster Press, 1971), p. 57.

fundamental demand of chastity: unconditional reverence for life, the *whole* of life, including genital feelings. People who avoid personal relations by repressing feelings separate tenderness (affectivity) from the whole of life. Infatuated people never do so, for the integrating power of eros will not permit such a separation.

Repressed people, regardless of the object of their repression, are idolatrous. Persons whom they encounter are not persons to be accepted in loving openness, but objects to be either avoided or feared. Anxious preoccupation with the isolated genital sexual aspect of human encounter destroys the repressed person's ability to make a free, open, rich, tender, warm, gentle encounter with anyone, most especially with those who appear as sexed others, whether they be of the same or opposite sex.

By denying their bodies and their feelings, repressed people deny the possibility of being intimate, because intimacy is an experience of being *wholly* and deeply touched by others. Interpersonal mystery, especially the mystery that can be revealed through our male or female bodies, has been forced out of the lives of repressed persons. To them, the work of creation, revealed through the fact of our embodiment, ceases to be a wonderful work of the Holy. Instead, it becomes a problem to be denied. Feelings, natural to the human body, must be eliminated. Genital feelings, the root of tenderness, must be ripped out. Consequently, repressed persons must avoid personal situations, for such situations always hold the possibility of a tender moment.

Repressed persons in positions of authority are seriously threatened by anyone who is infatuated, for infatuation is always an experience that contains a heightened awareness of our affective, sexual selves. In the infatuated person, the self of tenderness is beginning to emerge in the form of genital feelings. This budding self must be snipped, for its appearance is a painful reminder to repressed persons that they have cut off the possibility of their own growth in tenderness. Repressed persons in positions of authority promote community atmospheres as productive as deserts.

Through our bodies, we are able to become present and accessible to each other. Repressed people have become absent and inaccessible. They have become distracted by the denial of genital feelings. They cannot be interpersonally playful, for they must maintain a vigilant stance. They must guard against their own feelings and the feelings of others. They must filter all interpersonal utterances and behavior, and they must anxiously and continuously survey the landscape to insure that no one violates their sacred but unchaste taboo.

They deny and do not permit themselves to see anything that expresses human sexuality. Yet they stare and glare at sexual expression. Watts reminds us that vigilance of this sort fosters neither understanding nor acceptance, only strain[6] and, I would add, self-consciousness.

Repressed people are distracted. They are unable to husband the feelings of others. In their state of distraction, they are unable to contemplate the *here* and *now*. They are unable to have that clear vision of the present that permits and fosters singlemindedness. They are unable to be mindful that when genital feelings are properly cultivated, tenderness, lived out as respectful affection, is the inevitable result.

---

6. Watts, pp. 77ff.

In denying our feelings, we always throw ourselves into a confused, distracted, uncreative loneliness. Repressed persons are lonely people, and they avoid their loneliness by retreating into the material universe provided by the functional world, the world of work. There, their sterile attitude blends with the props of functional existence, and they are safe from the threat of interpersonal intimacy. They do not have to take the risk called for in Psalm 139. They do not have to expose themselves to the wonderful work of creation that is our incarnated human sexuality, the root that gives rise to the self of human affectivity. In the functional world, such persons are able to organize, manage, and control the messages that are revealed through feelings by filtering these messages through their own private code, a code that translates every message into the sterile language of efficiency.

FEELINGS AND THE CALL TO THE PERSONAL MODE OF EXISTENCE

It is a tragic irony that the interpersonal life of sexually promiscuous persons holds more promise of conversion to interpersonal holiness than that of repressed persons, for the former at least are in the presence of others. Because gentle human contact is possible for promiscuous persons, tenderness and personal encounter are also possible. Unconsciously, repressed persons are dimly aware of this fact and of the transcendent power that they ascribe to feelings, especially genital feelings. Thus they are often very depressed. Their depression is best understood as a sense of loss. They are grieving for something that is rooted deep in human nature, something that comes alive within us and is evoked in the presence of other human beings: the call to personhood. Their too severe pruning has prevented them from hearing this call.

Repressed persons feel the call to personhood in the manner that deaf persons might feel vibrations. They feel a deep longing, an urgent longing that is a desire for an absent someone or something. But repressed persons are unable to respond. By getting rid of genital feelings, they have gotten rid of tenderness and the possibility of personal contact. Infatuated people, on the other hand, hear the call to personhood. They simply misunderstand its message. In their impetuosity, they err in the opposite direction. Because they are lonely, they feel an urgent need for acceptance and understanding. Yet they cannot grasp that this urgency either drives people away or invites fantasy relationships.

Infatuated people are trying to answer a call to be separate, unique beings; their hearts instruct them to seek the beloved. They answer a call occasioned by a desire to be seen, known, and responded to as whole individuals, as persons. They desire to be known on the personal level; they know that when tender care, concern, and respect are absent, relationships become anonymous and impersonal. The call to personhood must be answered in a creative way, one that cultivates the possibility of integration. Obviously, the repressed person's approach is too severe. It does not cultivate the emerging self of tenderness; it plows it under. Such an approach does not let love's journeymen even glance at an *ignis fatuus.*

Disciplined, informed knowing is the only avenue open to those of us who feel a sense of commitment to infatuated persons. If we are to tell the story of intimacy properly, we must be aware of the profound emotional importance of genital feelings. If erotic urgency is to be transformed into respectful tenderness, those responsible for husbanding others must be willing to share their wisdom concerning intimacy and authentic genital encounter. Infatuated persons must be guided away from the voices of repression. They must be invited to listen to their genital feelings in a more patient, quiet, respectful way. Perhaps they might be taught about what their urgent longings impel them to seek. Such instruction does not necessarily encourage action; it simply teaches that the call to genital intimacy is a call to a deeper communion.

INTIMACY AND AUTHENTIC GENITAL ENCOUNTER

In the first moment of an authentic genital encounter, each person discovers that the other's body reacts differently from his own. Adrian van Kaam teaches us that each body is the incarnation of a different biological, cultural, and psychological heritage. Each person must be faithful to that heritage if the encounter is to be an authentic personal one. For example, if naturally phlegmatic, introverted persons try to act as if they are more energetic and extroverted, they will be doing violence to who and what they are.[7]

As the genital encounter unfolds, each partner accommodates himself to the other. If the encounter is authentic, the mutual accommodation is such that each remains faithful to self. The partners do not change places. They

7. Adrian van Kaam, "A Psychology of Man and Woman," unpublished lecture notes, Duquesne University, 1964. See also idem, "Sex and Existence," *Review of Existential Psychology and Psychiatry* 2 (1963): 163-81.

do not abandon their separate selves. Rather, each participates in the other's temperament and style. This experience is most mysterious and is characterized as a kind of dance. The partners literally explore each other, but their gentle, tender searching-to-please is done in a manner that is respectfully attuned to both partner and self. Each is careful to caress in a way that is acceptable in order to avoid being exploitive.

As the dance continues, each person moves in response to the other in a manner that heightens the other's pleasure, until both, in turn or simultaneously, undergo a moment of excitement during which they get lost in each other, when their bodies surrender to each other. This moment is followed by a moment of quiet, of peace, of satisfied sadness.

In that moment they discover experientially that they have been called out of the depth of solitude to be completed and complemented by another person. They discover that in the midst of their act their existence did not evaporate but was *en*countered.[8] They discover that their bodily being has been called and met by an other who cares. Dietrich von Hildebrand speaks of this discovery as a moment of mutual self-donation.[9] In such a moment we discover that the solitude we are, by virtue of being sexed,[10] recedes into the background and that the possi-

---

8. More will be said of the experience of being *en*countered in subsequent chapters.

9. Dietrich von Hildebrand, *Man and Woman* (Chicago: Franciscan Herald Press, 1966).

10. For a more thorough explication of man as a sexed being, see Maurice Merleau-Ponty, *The Phenomenology of Perception* (New York: Humanities Press, 1962).

bility of communion *with* and *through* others is affirmed. Through the value of respect lived out as tender care and concern, we go beyond intimacy toward communion, and we participate in a personal moment that generally eludes those who try to make love happen.

This story of authentic genital intimacy teaches us to be faithful to our own and others' style and temperament. It teaches that the movement toward others emerges from our own one-sidedness, that the need for human intimacy can be satisfied but never fulfilled, and, most importantly, that to be loving we must be ourselves. This story should dwell on the moment of satisfied sadness, for it teaches us that the movement toward a moment of genital intimacy is indeed a hunger for something more. The story also teaches us to expect disappointment, for authentic human intimacy heightens our awareness of human limits. The story assures infatuated persons that their search can never be satisfied through genital expression.

INFATUATION PROMOTES SEXUAL INTEGRATION

It is most important for us to learn to differentiate the affective sexual from the genital mode of human existence. But these modes can be separated in a way that strangles the possibility of moving from homogenital or hetero-genital urgency toward affectivity. Repression always promotes the split. Awareness and respectful acceptance always promote the possibility of integration.[11]

---

11. This point will be addressed more fully in subsequent chapters.

Infatuated persons are unable to differentiate genital urgency and affectivity. Repressed persons are likewise handicapped, but in denying the genital they kill off the possibility of transforming genital urgency into respectful love. They "kill" because they commit an act of violence; they violate interpersonal holiness. They frustrate the Holy Spirit as it calls them to witness through their sexuality.

Repressed people fail to allow genital urgency the opportunity to emerge, grow to maturity, and propagate its seeds of interiority. They objectify genital feeling, splitting it off from the whole of human existence. But infatuated persons do not have to participate in this violence. The story of authentic genital intimacy will spare them the violence of repression and might spare them their own violence. From it they will learn the affective ideal, an ideal that asks for risk, openness, and surrender. They will learn that the call to genital intimacy is always a call to love, to be respectfully tender and patiently gentle with someone for whom they care. If they should answer the call genitally, they have to be treated as disappointed people who in their disappointment will seek isolation and will express resentment toward their beloved.

INFATUATION FORESHADOWS
CONTEMPLATIVE AWARENESS

Infatuated persons must learn that interpersonal tenderness and gentleness are possible only if a contemplative attitude accompanies personal relationship. They must learn that tenderness and gentleness are emotions (L. *e* = out + *movere* = to move), not mere feelings; they are feelings that orient, that *move* us toward a particular kind of relationship. They should know about their genital feelings, which can remain fixated, attached to the biological, confined to the bodily level of solitary human existence. Persons who are thus genitally fixated can lead interpersonal lives that are either homogenital or heterogenital in orientation. Either mode of relating remains stuck at the level of urgency and fosters a life of constant agitation.

Kraft teaches that persons who displace love with sex are driven people who are constantly in search of new bodies and thrills to satisfy their drives. Their fixation on the immediacy of sex forces them to always find new bodies. But they are unconsciously searching for transcendent love in their exploits. Unfortunately, their futile attempts never let them find what they really desire, for they have asked sex to be the Holy.[12] Genitally active people must be made to see that persons who displace love with sex cannot take up the contemplative attitude, for they are too agitated, too restless. They cannot still the noise within their minds nor the desperate urgency within their hearts. They are too full of themselves. They cannot empty their minds and quiet their hearts. Watts says that such people are constantly engaged in fighting off a sense of boredom or depression; are agitated and afraid; seek to get the most out of their pleasure; and are driven by a compulsion to be loving, attentive, patient, or happy.[13] Such persons cannot realize that moment Zen Buddhism calls *satori,* "the effortless, spontaneous, and sudden dawning of realization,"[14] the moment of awareness Christian mystics call *contemplation,* the moment of emergence fostered by husbanding.

12. Kraft, pp. 155-56.
13. Watts, p. 77.
14. Ibid.

When a relationship focuses only on the genital aspect of human intimacy, it fails to foster that attitude that permits both lovers and small children to sit by a lake and gaze in wonder at a leaf as it mysteriously floats on the water's surface.

Repressed people cannot achieve awareness, but they do regard the urgency of infatuation with a bit of wisdom. They realize that genital intimacy can be a need that binds, that robs lovers of their freedom, making the desire for love become a demand. Unfortunately, repressed persons attempt to apply this wisdom in the manner of the headache victim who seeks to eliminate pain by decapitation. The next chapter focuses on this sense of urgency, which seems to frighten repressed persons into lives of denial for themselves and others. The chapter attempts to bring the wisdom of repression out of its shadow existence into the daylight where it belongs.

III

HUMAN LOVE: THE NEED THAT BINDS

Slow-paced I come,
Yielding by inches.
And yet, oh Lord, and yet,
—Oh Lord, let not likeness fool me again.

C. S. Lewis
Sweet Desire

Those who attempt to frustrate or deny the infatuation experience might be inspired by the wisdom that the urgency of infatuation moves people toward idolatry. Perhaps they are even motivated by the maxim of St. John, that only "God is Love." My experience with both repressive and repressed people suggests that most of them are simply threatened by the genital urgency of infatuation. Yet their vision, with its lack of reverence, does perceive that infatuated people do ask the beloved to be God for them. In charity, I would like to think that repressive people are trying to avert the inevitable resentment that results when someone is asked to be God, a request that no mortal can ever hope to fulfill. Repressive people may be expressing their own disappointment. The story of human intimacy must include the voices of repression, which should be heard with compassion and discernment.

THE IDOLATRY OF HUMAN LOVE

C. S. Lewis sheds some light on what repressive people may be wanting to express through their anxious fear: "Every human love at its height has a tendency to claim for itself a divine authority. Its voice tends to sound as if it were the will of God Himself. It tells us not to count the cost, it demands of us a total commitment, it attempts to over-ride all other claims and insinuates that any action which is sincerely done for love's sake is thereby lawful and even meritorious."[1] Lewis knows the problem of infatuation. He knows that the experience is riddled with self-sacrificing passion, an altruism that can be idolatrous because it speaks to us with what seems to be the voice of God. However, unlike repressive people, Lewis is not threatened by the urgency of human love: "A faithful and genuinely self-sacrificing passion will speak to us with what seems to be the voice of God. Merely animal or frivolous lust will not. It will corrupt its addict in a dozen ways, but not in that way; a man may act upon such feelings but he cannot *revere* them any more than a man who scratches reveres the itch."[2]

Yet Lewis is able to see that love's altruism does tend to act as if it possessed divine authority. Lewis seems to know that human love is not really able to be entirely unselfish, but, unlike repressive people, he is not intimidated by human lust. Lewis and repressive people, however, do share the belief that human love poses a major problem because it can fascinate us, attaching us to the love object

---

1. C. S. Lewis, *The Four Loves* (New York: Harcourt, Brace, Jovanovich, 1960), p. 18.

2. Ibid. [Italics added.]

in a way that we become blind to St. John's maxim that *"God* is Love." Human love as defined by Lewis always tends to displace the real thing, such that the thing we love on the human level inevitably becomes the thing we control.

At first we might be tempted to accept the perverted wisdom of the repressive. Human love can indeed claim a divine authority over its adherents. But echoing St. John of the Cross, Lewis instructs us that our human fascinations only possess the power to captivate us because there is in them "a real resemblance to God, to Love Himself." Lewis continues: "Let us make no mistake. . . . Our Gift-loves [infatuation] . . . are really God-like; and among our Gift-loves, those are most God-like which are most boundless and unwearied in giving. All the things the poets say about them are true. Their joy, their energy, their patience, their readiness to forgive, their desire for the good of the beloved—all this is a real and all but adorable image of the Divine life. In its presence we are right to thank God 'who has given such power to men.' We may say, quite truly and in an intelligible sense, that those who love greatly are 'near' to God."[3] Lewis offers a rather sharp retort to those who seek to interfere with the gift of infatuation; in effect, he suggests that they should not mind God's business, but their own.

Lewis has the intuitive knowledge of infatuated people. He seems to know that human love can gather about itself a splendor that can evoke awe and wonder. He knows it can call us up and out of ourselves. But he also knows that human love tends to possess a natural narcissism that moves us to dominate the object of our desire. Those out-

---

3. Ibid., p. 19.

side the circle of love witness this narcissism; they observe the possessive, demanding quality of the relationship. They feel the pressure and distance imposed by the lovers' intense reverence for each other. They observe love's idolatry. Yet Lewis assures us that there is something of God in all this.

But how are we to rescue persons from the potential idolatry of infatuation? Current psychological thinking would advise us either to let the thing run its course or to get people involved in creative activity, i.e., to sublimate. In view of what has been said already, sublimation would seem to be only another form of repression. Integrity would dictate that we follow the first advice, which requires us to be open to the imitating and idolatrous aspects of the experience. Is it possible to heed the message of repression without moving in the direction of severity? Is it possible to bring affectivity to fruition while accommodating the negative and disruptive aspects of infatuation?

Classical mystical literature can help us answer these questions. The mystics were attuned to the integration of the human and the Holy. They sought to ground their spiritual life in human experience. They also sought to ground their human life in the Spirit. For example, the spiritual poetry of St. John of the Cross chronicles his own journey to loving intimacy with Love Himself. The poetry offers a diary of his experience, an autobiography of an orphan in search of a home. It is the story of his spiritual adolescence as he sought to grow beyond infatuation toward intimate knowing with Love Himself. While the story's imagery may seem strange, it does address the experience of infatuation.

The following verses are from "The Dark Night," which
is reprinted in its entirety in Appendix A.

1. One dark night,
    Fired with love's urgent longings
    —Ah, the sheer grace!—
    I went out unseen,
    My house being now all stilled;

    . . . .

5. O guiding night!
    O night more lovely than the dawn!
    O night that has united
    The Lover with His beloved,
    Transforming the beloved in her Lover.

6. Upon my flowering breast
    Which I kept wholly for Him alone,
    There He lay sleeping,
    And I caressing Him
    There in a breeze from the fanning cedars.

    . . . .

8. I abandoned and forget myself,
    Laying my face on my Beloved;
    All things ceased; I went out from myself,
    Leaving my cares
    Forgotten among the lilies.

There is the idealization of love in this poem; there is a
being in love with Love; there is all the joy, splendor, and
fascination that characterize those encounters we call loving. To again quote Lewis: "Their joy, their energy, their
patience, their readiness to forgive, their desire for the
good of the beloved—all this is a real and all but adorable

image of the Divine life. . . . Those who love greatly are 'near' to God. But of course it is 'nearness by likeness.'"

INFATUATION'S URGENCY:
A PATHWAY TO POVERTY

It goes without saying that St. John of the Cross loves God, and it would appear that his road to sanctity began with an enthusiasm that was fired by urgency. The story of human intimacy teaches us that the urgency of infatuation is a pathway to contemplative intimacy. Perhaps this pathway can become more clear if we reflect on our own experience.

In that very special reciprocal relationship we call first love, did we not feel we were being pulled toward our loved ones? Did they not awaken a feeling of awe? Did they not seem to walk in mystery? Did not their very presence, or the mere suggestion of that presence, overtake our own intentions, perhaps making us more graceful or more clumsy than we were? Did they not radiate magic? Were we not moved toward ecstacy by their smiles, their touches, any of their ingratiating gestures? Did we not come to a heightened, though perhaps overly solicitous, awareness of their flaws *and* their gifts? Were we not united in wonder and reverence? Did we not desire to serve our loved ones in willing obedience with no desire for reciprocity?

When we recall our own experience of infatuation, we can appreciate how St. John of the Cross feels in his dark night poem. We feel deeply and spontaneously moved to abandon our self-centered interests, to become invisible to ourselves and "go out unseen." We feel called to center ourselves in the other, to "still our own house." Infatuation, like St. John's experience of his Beloved, tends to call us to be singleminded. It tends to claim a power over our attention such that our individuality gets lost. But an infatuated encounter is not thereby an authentic encounter. Authentic encounter involves identification and opposition, both of which are lacking in the experience of infatuation.[4] Our self-sacrificing passion promotes a curious blindness to our sense of selfhood whereby our own singularity stands out in clear relief. These moments of "going beyond ourselves," these moments in which we feel called "up" and "out" of ourselves, foster a sense of ecstacy and reverence that makes the presence of the other feel like the presence of the Holy and makes our presence diminish to the point of disappearance.

How are we rescued from this thing that Lewis calls our inclination to "give our human loves the unconditional allegiance which we owe only God"?[5] St. John of the Cross provides us with a clue when he speaks of the dark night experience, that painful experience when we feel the loss or separation from our Beloved.

At some point in the experience of first love (even if it is being experienced the tenth time), the idolized one begins to feel the pressure of being needed. It is often at the height of such pressure that the lovers give themselves over to the urgency of their genital feelings. Moreover, often it is on the heels of such experiences that the lovers find that being needed genitally robs them of their personal freedom, of their independence. It is at this point that infatuated persons are awakened to the wisdom that they cannot be God,

---

4. Rolf von Eckartsburg, "Encounter as the Basic Unit of Social Interaction," *Humanitas* 2 (Fall 1965): 197.

5. Lewis, p. 19.

and they inevitably pull back. With this distance comes a feeling of separation that is unacceptable. The distance echoes a feeling of other losses and inevitably makes the needy person feel threatened. At this point, infatuated persons generally reassert the claim they have upon the beloved.

St. John's poem entitled "The Spiritual Canticle" wisely shows us what happens after the moment of being "fired with love's urgent longings." In the first stanza, the bride complains about her absent lover:

> 1. Where have you hidden,
>   Beloved, and left me moaning?
>   You fled like the stag
>   After wounding me;
>   I went out calling You, and You were gone.[6]

The bride is suffering the loss of her beloved. She feels lost, abandoned. She begins to wander about in a state of utter confusion:

> 2. Shepherds, you that go
>   Up through the sheepfolds to the hill,
>   If by chance you see
>   Him I love most
>   Tell Him that I sicken, suffer, and die.

Her lament continues throughout the soliloquy, but the closing stanzas of the bride's monologue shift in tone:

> 9. Why, since You wounded
>   This Heart, don't You heal it?

---

6. St. John of the Cross, *The Collected Works of St. John of the Cross,* trans. Kieran Kavanaugh and Otilio Rodriguez (Washington, DC: Institute of Carmelite Studies Publications, 1973). This poem is reprinted in Appendix B.

And why, since You stole it from me,
Do You leave it so,
And fail to carry off what You have stolen?

10. Extinguish these miseries,
Since no one else can stamp them out;
And may my eyes behold You,
Because You are their light,
And I would open them to You alone.

11. Reveal Your presence
And may the vision of Your beauty be my death;
For the sickness of love
Is not cured
Except by Your very presence and image.

The withdrawal of her loved one has left a sense of loss and resentment that the bride experiences as an urgency to be reunited. But the urgency is met by silence, a heavy, ponderous silence to which she responds with confusion, doubt, anxiety, loneliness, depression, and the bitterness of resentment. The experience of separation or loss always involves these feelings, for they are love's poverty.

Those of us who have undergone the experience of first love can recall being fired by urgency. We can also recall the negative feelings that always accompany the withdrawal or absence of the beloved. Indeed, throughout our lives, the loss of someone or something that we value is always accompanied by pain. When we lose something with which or someone with whom we have been fascinated, the loss is all the more acute. When the fascinating object or person is no longer available, the emotional claim that it made upon our lives is felt with a pain whose intensity borders on agony, a "dark night."

In "The Spiritual Canticle," the bride suffers the loss of her beloved. As she "suffers, sickens, and dies," she does a fair amount of complaining. She *demands* his return. She *insists* that because of her pain he should return, "*reveal* his presence," "*heal* her heart," "*extinguish* her miseries," *do* something. She has been touched by love. Her beloved's absence promotes pain, and in expressing that pain she reveals the expectations and demands that attend love, *human* love, when it springs from possessiveness, the affective state of fascination we call infatuation. She exclaims, "You have touched me in love," "I had you," "You are gone," "I'm in pain," and she insists that her love *do* something about it. She is "fascinated" with love. The bride is fastened, attached, fused, to her beloved. Without him, she is immobilized, frozen in her *need* of him. Her sentiments echo those of infatuated people, especially when they have been active genitally.

From the bride's point of view, the beloved, her groom, holds her in his grasp. But from the groom's perspective, the meaning of the situation is curiously different. Her love for him is a clingy, possessive kind of love. She will not let her lover go; her life *depends* on his presence. In her clinging, possessive state she is *demanding* his presence, saying he has no right to leave her. Although she is dependent, her complaints reveal that her love is also a kind of domination. She insists that her lover return to gratify the demands of her love. We therefore must not be seduced by her pain, for as Charles Maes tells us, persons who seek to have their need for love gratified are really seeking to dominate![7] St. John of the Cross shows us that the bride's

7. Charles Maes, unpublished lectures on psychoanalysis, Duquesne University, Pittsburgh, Pennsylvania, March 10, 1976.

urgent longing really betrays dependent need. In seeking to be comforted, in seeking to have her pain alleviated, she is really seeking to dominate and control her beloved. She is seeking to *make* him the source of satisfaction. He is the *object* of an urgent desire for comfort, warmth, and security. Listening to her whining and sniveling, we can readily understand the inclination of repressive people to prune too severely.

It is quite clear that the bride's attitude toward her beloved must undergo a transformation. She needs to be liberated from the urgency of her need. But before we are tempted to give in to the repressive point of view, we must remember Lewis's advice. We must see how "near to Love" this clingy possessiveness really is. As Lewis reminds us, we must see how near to God this state of dependent need really is. If we do not see, we might be overwhelmed by the bride's urgency, and we might move in the direction of repressing the experience in order to rescue her from its heresy.

The story of human intimacy is reflected in "The Dark Night" and "The Spiritual Canticle." St. John of the Cross wants us to recognize that the human experience of love is rooted in human need. He wants us to see that in being "fired with love's urgent longings" we are moved immediately to seek gratification. He wants us to see that infatuated persons, like the bride of the canticle, want the beloved to *"make* them feel good." He wants us to see that this bursting forth in enthusiasm, this being "fired with love's urgent longings," promotes a fusion with the beloved that robs infatuated persons of their freedom to choose. He wants us to see that the urgency of infatuation moves us to a kind of reckless self-abandonment that promotes a peculiar form of idolatry, one that robs us of our freedom and, as a consequence, of our identity.

GRATIFICATION SEEKS
TO AVOID LIFE'S POVERTY

St. John is aware of the problem posed by love's urgency. Yet, in spite of his understanding of the idolatry of infatuation, he is not moved toward repression. Rather, his spiritual theology, both in "The Ascent of Mount Carmel" and "The Spiritual Canticle,"[8] affirms the reality and validity of the urgency of infatuation. He apprehends the wisdom of repressive persons. He sees the need for transformation, and in response to this need he introduces a rule, the rule of abstinence. Actually, this rule is more a rhythm of denial and respectful participation, what Adrian van Kaam refers to as the life rhythm of involvement and detachment.[9] We observe this rhythm in both "The Dark Night" and "The Spiritual Canticle." In the latter, the beloved is absent whereas in the former the lovers are united. Toward the conclusion of the latter, the lovers are reunited, but the relationship is less tempestuous, less urgent. Desire has been tempered by separation, and it allows for more freedom and choice in the relationship.

However, the rule of abstinence is often interpreted as a killing off of desire, through total *avoidance* and *denial*. In his spiritual theology, St. John speaks of the first "dark night" as being the "dark night of the senses," but he

---

8. *Collected Works,* pp. 65-291; 391-565.

9. Adrian van Kaam, *On Being Involved* (Wilkes Barre, PA: Dimension Books, 1970).

never speaks of killing the senses. The rule of abstinence is not a technique to commit violence. It is a means of liberation from the fascinations that promote our natural human inclination to dominate others, particularly when we are threatened by the loss of something we feel we need. The elimination of pleasure, satisfaction, and celebration is not at issue for St. John. At issue is the state of being fastened and the expectations and demands that flow from fascination. At issue is a fusion, a desire to cling to others when we feel threatened, a desire that is wholly in the service of dominance. St. John of the Cross says: "The fly that clings to honey hinders its flight, and the soul that allows itself attachment to spiritual sweetness hinders its own liberty and contemplation."[10] At issue here is the urgency and dominance revealed in the bride's need for gratification, a need to which she is apparently oblivious.

The bride, at the beginning of the canticle, like an infatuated adolescent, seeks to be gratified. But neither the bride nor infatuated persons can dwell in that reverential attitude that allows them to *enjoy* the beloved. Searching for gratification is not the same as allowing oneself to be surprised by joy. Those who seek gratification are rather like Lewis before his conversion to Theism; they seek joy or pleasure as an end. They are unable to appreciate that joy points beyond itself to a larger and deeper reality. Infatuated persons are desperate for joyful moments. But they do not have the wisdom to see that their desperate longing for joy makes it elude their grasp.

The attitude in which joy is an end is visible to novice masters or mistresses whose charges have fallen in love

---

10. *Collected Works*, p. 668.

with them. They report that their novices begin to feel that
they at long last have found someone who understands
these powerful feelings that have been creating such confusion; they undergo an experience of "feeling really understood." However, the ecstasy that initially flows from such
an experience occasions a hunger for further understanding with its attendant joy. A curious thing begins to occur:
the hunger itself begins to be an urgency to be understood.
The longing itself becomes an urgency, a deep, consuming
need to be understood. Unfortunately but inevitably, the
joy the novices first experienced soon becomes a sadness
and then a disappointment. Under the pressure of such
urgent need, the persons who are objects of that need withdraw, and the novices consequently begin to perceive
themselves as social failures. They conclude that others
cannot understand them because they are unworthy of being understood, accepted, or loved.

These feelings, in fact, are not totally inaccurate. Others
really cannot enter into the kind of relationship the novices
need at that moment. To do so willingly would be to allow
themselves to be totally dominated. The search for joy, in
this case the joy of being understood, is really a desire to
possess total and perfect understanding. In their search the
novices are like the bride of the canticle, who, having been
touched by love, develops a consuming need to be gratified
by love. As we observed in the poem, her search for
gratification is really a will-to-dominate the original source
of her pleasure. The enjoyment and freedom of love escape
her grasp.

So it is with those who are first touched by an understanding other; they are fired by an urgent longing whose
urgency promotes a dark night. The one who has brought

light into their lives, be it the light of understanding, acceptance, or whatever, withdraws under pressure of their urgent need to maintain the light, and when the beloved withdraws, they feel themselves to be left in darkness. Life ceases to provide enjoyment; they feel imprisoned, unable to choose; the choice of either freedom or enjoyment is no longer available, and they dwell in darkness.

Paul Ricoeur instructs us that gratification and dominance are opposed to enjoyment and freedom.[11] St. John of the Cross offers the same wisdom. As long as we are fastened to love, caught up in the search for love, we are infatuated; we are dominated by our *need* for love's splendor. Consequently, the governing principle of life is twofold: (1) to be constantly gratified and (2) to avoid the pain that comes from separation or loss. When we live according to what Maes calls the "rule of gratification," we always experience the *urgency* to be pleased, to be gratified. We always feel the urgency to seek pleasure. When we live according to the rule of gratification, we cannot abide being separated. We cannot tolerate the absence of the love object.

The rule of abstinence, however, although clearly a staying away from, a withdrawal, is more of a separation in service of acknowledgment, a poverty in service of growth. We *choose* not to have the objects of our desire in order to grow more deeply in *reverence* of them. The rule of abstinence introduces into the consciousness of infatuated persons the dying of desire, the death of urgency. Maes notes: "Only that desire that has accepted its own death is

---

11. Paul Ricoeur, *Freud and Philosophy: An Essay on Interpretation* (New Haven, CT: Yale University Press, 1970).

truly free.'' *Only when we can freely choose the objects of our desire are we free from the glue of fascination.* Only when we are simultaneously free to let the objects of our desire choose us and to let ourselves choose them are we free from the need to be gratified. But such an attitude can be fostered only when we surrender to life's poverty, and this surrender is precisely what infatuated persons cannot permit.

THE RULE OF ABSTINENCE PROMOTES LIBERATION

When we interpret St. John's rule of abstinence as a relinquishing, we are referring to gratification. We are saying that abstinence *imposes* deprivation. We are like the bride and the infatuated person, for whom life means feeling gratified, for whom identity is dependent on the presence of that other who gratifies their need, be it a need for acceptance, for understanding, or to be loved.

St. John of the Cross knows that when we avoid recognizing the things to which we are attached—people, money, understanding, acceptance, sexual pleasure—we also avoid the transforming, liberating pain of real detachment. He knows that in the state of infatuation the pain we experience during a period of separation is occasioned by our level of fascination. The greater the fascination, the more intense the need. Consequently, the more acutely we experience the pain of absence.

When we read "The Spiritual Canticle," we are "caught in the act." St. John of the Cross knows that we will focus on the pain of absence, that we will focus on the bride's need. He knows that, like repressives, we tend to live by the pleasure deprivation rule. St. John of the Cross introduces the rule of abstinence in order to reeducate our hearts. He wants to reorient desire from urgent need to appreciation. He does not want us to be indifferent to the bride's complaint. He wants us to identify with it in order that we might be reeducated. In his beautiful poem, he instructs us emotionally; he lets us *feel* the groom's absence. He wants us to *feel* the bride's clinging desire, her dependence. He wants to tell us to loosen ourselves from the honey of urgent need. He knows, as Maes has said, that the deepest fear of the dependent self is to lose the source of its pleasure. In faith, St. John of the Cross says let go, allow the groom to return at his leisure when he deems it appropriate. He wants us to allow the groom to be *free* to return.

St. John of the Cross would offer a practical wisdom to novices and all persons who are infatuated. He would affirm that their urgent longing for understanding, acceptance, or love is indeed fired by a profound desire that must be expressed. But he would quietly remind them that at first this desire will be expressed as an urgent need. Confronted with such urgency, the object of the need—the beloved—will have to withdraw, for the loved one will feel pressured to satisfy the need. In the face of such pressure, loved ones will have to withdraw to protect their integrity, their freedom to choose, and, indeed, their very identity. The story of human intimacy teaches that urgency has the potential to distort the reality of the human other by conferring the power to provide absolute fulfillment. In the face of the demand for fulfillment, mortal lovers must flee in integrity or surrender to an illusion that will rob them of their mortal identity. Real lovers must flee from the urgency of love, for they know "urgency" acts like honey pouring itself over their freedom to respond to love.

But because the urgency of infatuation promotes a deafness similar to that of repression, not everyone can hear this story of human intimacy. Infatuated persons will hear only bothersome vibrations. Yet we must not lose the patient openness with which we tell the story; to do so is to fall sway to the voices of repression. We must continue to try to husband the experience of infatuated persons. We must listen to this experience in the hope that its urgent inventions of the heart will contain their own seeds of transformation, seeds that will lend themselves to proper husbandry.

The next chapter focuses on the process of detachment from these urgent inventions of the heart. It offers the voices of repression an alternative to the avoidance or denial of infatuation. It addresses the issue of affective transformation and the emergence of freedom.

IV

LONELINESS AND
THE TRANSFORMED SELF

To be loved means to be consumed,
To love is to give light with inexhaustible oil.
To be loved is to pass away,
To love is to endure.

Rainer Maria Rilke

Rainer Maria Rilke's remarks on love indict infatuation, pointing to the fundamental error of the experience.[1] Lovers long to endure forever, but infatuated people are most reluctant to "pass away" or "be consumed"; while they long to give themselves in loving surrender, they also desire to cling to the beloved. They want to keep their gaze fixed on the beloved forever. They want to see the beloved as someone who will constantly fulfill their urgent longing for love. Their inventions of the heart spring from this desire. Yet, even in the midst of imagining the lover as perfect, they feel something missing.

In an article entitled "Chastening of Love," Julia Norton articulates the missing dimension. For Norton, love is

---

1. Rainer Maria Rilke, *The Notebooks of Malte, Laurice Brigge,* trans. M. D. Herter Morton (New York: Norton, 1964), p. 209.

not love unless it is respectful, and it is not respectful in the Christian sense unless it also embraces "death." She reminds us that in the Christian sense we answer the call to respectful love when we share in Christ's passion, death, and resurrection.[2] Infatuated persons cannot tolerate such a vision because it is too immersed in human weakness. They cannot accept weakness of any sort.

INFATUATION: A FALSE VISION

The refusal of infatuated persons to accept personal faults or limits makes them basically disrespectful. They may be reverent witnesses for the beloved, but their reverence is not grounded on respect for the reality of others, *with* their limits, *in* their mortality. Infatuated love is disrespectful because it falsifies the human existence of the beloved. If infatuated persons feel bitter, lost, confused, and in need of understanding and acceptance, they perceive the loved one as *perfectly* accepting and understanding. For example, we need only recall Catherine of Emily Bronte's *Wuthering Heights* when she meets and falls in love with Heathcliff, or Dante when he met Beatrice.

By transforming human limits or flaws into something positive, creative, or beautiful, infatuated persons in turn transform reality into illusion. In this way, they circumvent the dying, the consummation, the passing away that Rilke and Norton tell us is immanent to love. In infatuation the beloved is transformed by and into an illusion of perfection.

How does this illusion of perfection occur? What is the remedy? The transformation of reality into illusion of per-

---

2. Julia Norton, "Chastening of Love," *Envoy* 11 (March 1974): 1.

fection is brought about by a rather fundamental attitude all humans embrace. Adrian van Kaam speaks of this attitude as the poetic, or feminine, mode of existence. He refers to it as a fundamental, orienting attitude, taken up by both male and female.[3] I prefer the term *mythopoeisis*, for it exemplifies the way in which this poetic stance is lived in the interpersonal myth making of infatuation.[4]

Infatuated people need to make sense of where they have been. But the pressure of their urgent longings also creates in them a need to know where they are going. In particular, they need to know that the road ahead is safe. Because they are frightened, they take a poetic stance, and they invent. They try to sing a new reality into existence, one that eliminates all negative and unpleasant feelings, especially loneliness.

Infatuated persons who dwell in the poetic mode are at first faithful to reality, but their urgency and fear do not permit them to remain creatively faithful for long. After the first moment of naive, open perception, they are overtaken by romantic yearning. The park bench on which they may be sitting is romanticized into a bench of long ago on

---

3. Adrian van Kaam, "A Psychology of Man and Woman," unpublished lecture, Duquesne University, Pittsburgh, Pennsylvania, February 16, 1969.

4. The term is taken from the Greek words *mythos* (myth), a traditional truth revealing supernatural events employed to orient, guide, and direct natural events, and *poeisis* (singing into existence: creation). *Poeisis* is the root of the English word poesy, meaning poetic inspiration. I use the term *mythopoeisis* to convey the sense of being inspired to such a point of enthusiasm that we literally "sing" a reality into existence. Our presence to reality is then transformed, and our behavior is altered, redirected, or otherwise reoriented.

which they first sat beside a loved one and felt love's gentle touch.The past commands their attention, animating the present with its ghostly images. The images assume both a fullness and a power that they perhaps did not possess in the original experience.

Urgent need for an absent lover does tend to make moments of past satisfaction assume the breadth and depth of longed-for fulfillment. The urgent longing becomes a nostalgic longing. Nostalgia always instructs us that at one time in our lives perfection, fulfillment, and unity were all ours. Nostalgia instructs us that we were once fulfilled. But the romantic yearning of infatuation seeks to make the memory become the immediate reality. The past and the present are fused such that their witness to immediate reality is blurred by fantasy.

Ernest Becker speaks of the urgency of infatuation, suggesting that out of this need, which he calls "romantic," man gives witness to a need for "cosmic heroism . . . [which he fixes] . . . on to *another person* in the form of a love object . . . the love partner becomes the divine ideal within which to fulfill one's life. All spiritual and moral needs now become focused in one individual. . . . Salvation itself is no longer referred to an abstraction like God but can be sought in the beatification of the other."[5] Becker tells us that out of a need for transcendence, infatuated persons make their human loves the source of salvation, which nostalgia instructs was once theirs. Here the "law of gratification" is made to serve nostalgic longing. Infatuated persons need a god they can grasp. They need a

---

5. Ernest Becker, *The Denial of Death* (New York: The Free Press, 1973), p. 160.

god who can satisfy their immediate needs. Their human loves cannot be allowed to have flaws or imperfections; they must be perfect. Becker teaches us that because romantic illusion cannot allow flaws to appear, the beloved is beatified out of urgent need, a need promoted by nostalgic longing. The beloved is perceived as offering salvation, as offering the hope of permanence, endurance, and the avoidance of pain. The moment before infatuated persons are caught by their romantic yearnings, they are often reminded of the impermanence of immediate reality, they are aware that the present will pass away. This thought is threatening because it underlines their own vulnerability. In self-defense, they spin a "myth" of permanence. They are unaware that its web will entrap them and their human loves. The myth offers salvation from fear. To the extent that this salvation myth is mutual, infatuated persons instruct each other that they had better not be let down, that they had better give each other the thing that is wanted, or else a new myth will be invented. Nostalgic longing is a severe task master. The task is to avoid being "consumed" by that poverty that promotes real love.

How can the loved ones resist? In the relationship, their very identities rest upon an illusion created by their lovers, and, what is more to the point, either they conform to the illusion or their very existences are threatened. Inevitably, therefore, the loved ones withdraw from the pressure of urgency as the infatuated persons discover that the world of immediate reality will not order itself according to their urgent needs. They have an urgent need for warmth, comfort, and security. When their loved ones withdraw, the security blanket of illusion is torn away, and they are left cold, frightened, and alone. In their nostalgic urgency, they once again confront the poverty of immediate reality; fulfillment has escaped their grasp. Now they are alone. If they have been active genitally, they are not only alone but severely disappointed.

In their aloneness, however, they confront what van Kaam refers to as the fundamental feature of human sexuality: separation from others.[6] The root meaning of sex is the Latin *seco*, meaning to cut, or separate. The myth of Adam and Eve gives eloquent expression to this fundamental feature of human sexuality. It instructs us that we began as a unity, that we became sexed beings, separated from each other, and that after the Fall we came to live a life of mysterious isolation from but powerful attraction to each other and the source of our original unity. From this isolation flows a life of sorrow, which we are always striving to transcend. In essence, this myth can be viewed as a metaphor of divine experience, employed to teach us about ourselves and the Author of our life. The veracity of the myth might be viewed as the existential event that nostalgia seeks to restore to our immediate experience.

The anxiety and self-doubt of the infatuation experience rob us of the veracity of this story as an orienting myth, a myth that points to what *was* and what *is*. Mythopoeisis creates an alternative myth, one that teaches us that we are not Adam separated from Eve, both suffering in exile from each other and the Creator. Infatuated persons want to hear that their need for love can be fulfilled without having to experience pain, sorrow, or loneliness.

---

6. Van Kaam, unpublished lecture.

URGENT LONGING ORIGINATES
AS DEEP LONELINESS

The mythopoetic imagination takes nostalgic longing (what might be called our ontological human need for communion and unity with Love Himself) and fuses it with human, genital urgency. *It takes advantage of the fact that in our genital urgency we hear a promise of unity.* Mythopoeisis takes advantage of the urgent feeling of being drawn to the sexed other; it does so by promoting the illusion that our human loves can offer salvation from aloneness, can offer fulfillment, the fulfillment of perpetual intimacy, of "unity" restored. Here three basic human needs, the need for genital intimacy, the need for loving intimacy with someone who cares, and the need for original unity get painted into the same corner, the corner of genital urgency. Listening to the sweet song of romantic illusion, infatuated persons are more and more tempted to falsify reality. Their nostalgic longing promotes an increase in genital tension, and in their confused, lonely state, they begin to believe that the genital route is the road to love. They have been seduced by their refusal to accept loneliness.

Through the intensity of their urgent need, infatuated persons get stuck in the glue of passion. They are unable to detach themselves in order that they might learn that nostalgic longing is not a call to "respectfully love as Christ loved us."[7] Theirs is a denial of reality. In their beatification of the beloved, they deny the poverty of immediate reality; they deny death. Death, especially the

---

7. Norton, p. 1.

death of separation, is perceived by them as the barrier to communion with Perfection. They must deny all forms of death in an effort to make the immediate reality of the beloved endure forever. Thus they cannot hear the call to participate in Christ's passion, death, and resurrection.[8] By listening to the whisperings of the romantic seduction, they answer a call to falsify the immediate reality of human existence. They answer a call to numb the pain of loneliness, a pain that reminds us we live lives of separation, Adam separated from Eve. They participate in an illusion of intimacy, an illusion of salvation, an illusion of perfection, an illusion that makes them anesthetize the harsh reality of human sexuality as *seco,* separateness from each other and from our Original Source of unity.

There is, however, insight in these whispered illusions although, at the outset, it is an inarticulate insight. In the first blush of love, all that infatuated people are able to hear is their urgency. John Dunne suggests that initially this urgent nostalgic longing flows from "a deep loneliness . . . a longing for intimacy, for communion."[9] Dunne believes this longing seeks deeper intimacy, the intimacy of communion with God. But, he notes, "the longing itself does not know this, does not know that it longs for God."[10]

The longing is still trapped in human urgency. It is not yet transformed into that Love that allows deeper intimacy, the intimacy of communion. Oblivious to its real

---

8. Ibid.

9. John Dunne, *Reasons of the Heart* (New York: Macmillan, 1978), p. 58.

10. Ibid.

wisdom, it seeks other humans, and, like water that seeks its own level, it flows toward others who are hearing the same call. Infatuated people seek out each other. Each party literally stumbles onto the other. Theirs is not a relationship that begins out of free choice. They meet already enthused and fearful, and their enthusiasm disposes them to an excitement that is mutually intoxicating. They are so deliriously enthused that they do not see how carelessly they dispose of their independence. They get inebriated by an intimacy in which they are already participating before they even meet! Dunne believes that is an intimacy that has the potential of promoting communion with Love Himself, that the nostalgic urgency of infatuation carries within itself a longing for communion. C. S. Lewis appears to support this belief when he reminds us that there is nearness to God here. But if we are to consider these insights valid, we need a clue to their truthfulness. Proper husbandry needs the right seeds.

COMMUNION: URGENT LONGING TRANSFORMED

Ironically, the readiness with which infatuated people surrender to the romantic seduction provides a clue. They readily give themselves over to the myth of perfection and thus seek endurance in order to avoid the pain of deep loneliness. They seek intimacy with human beings, but in doing so they are trying desperately to avoid what Charles Cummings calls the desert of loneliness.[11] But in reality the deeper intimacy they seek, the nostalgic longing for communion with God spoken of by Dunne, escapes their

---

11. Charles Cummings, *Spirituality and the Desert Experience* (Denville, NJ: Dimension Books, 1978), pp. 42ff.

grasp. Thomas Merton is most eloquent on this issue, reminding us that as people of flesh we are easily seduced to a *downward* transcendence of emotionalism, sensualism, disquietude, discouragement, fear, and lust.[12] This downward transcendence, although it represents a search for communion, takes us in a direction that carries us away from the possibility of real communion, in the manner of an *ignis fatuus.* More intense loneliness is the inevitable result.

The voices of repression would tell infatuated persons to go the route of denial. But given the correctness of Dunne's vision, as well as contemporary psychological thought, it would appear that any attempt to interfere with infatuation would impede the natural unfolding of human nature. St. Thomas Aquinas would most likely frown upon such impediment as a tinkering with the work of Grace!

Although infatuated people might have to avoid, postpone, or perhaps deny certain behavior, they must not deny their experience, for it has the potential of promoting a poverty of loneliness, a poverty that St. John of the Cross believes is fertile ground for the Holy Spirit. "Love's urgent longings" do indeed send us out in "darkness." The nostalgic urgency of infatuation promotes in us an awareness that immediate reality is impoverished, that it cannot offer fulfillment, only satisfaction, and satisfaction is a momentary thing. The voices of repression know this. But neither debunking nor denial is the task of those who tell the story of human intimacy. They are called upon to invite infatuated persons to slow down and take their own

---

12. Thomas Merton, *New Seeds of Contemplation* (New York: New Directions Books, 1972), pp. 90-97.

experience seriously. When infatuated people undergo the pain of separation or the disappointment that is a natural part of human relationship, they experience the reality of life's poverty. Denial, or avoidance, cultivates a poverty of a different sort, one that does not serve growth.

INFATUATION: A SELF
IN GOD IN PROCESS

Ironically, there is a wisdom to the infatuation experience that will not allow interference. The experience has an integrity. It follows a flow of events that will not be averted. At the risk of being repetitious, I summarize that flow of events as follows: a feeling of being alone; a blush of excitement and enthusiasm in which two people feel spontaneously drawn to one another; a falling-in-love; and a being-in-love itself. In the being-in-love (with love) phase, the lovers' immaturity prohibits them from accepting and integrating negative features of their loved ones' personalities. The positive features of the beloved are seen with clarity and perceptiveness, but the negative features are falsified by a need for perfection. Thus there is both a real and an imagined presence to the beloved. The infatuated person literally flows back and forth between these two attitudes and is unable to distinguish between them. It is this back and forth movement that makes genital tension increase, putting pressure on the lovers and bringing about the final phase of infatuation, when the lovers must part from illusion, or each other.

The seeds of transformation are contained in the first and last phases: in the deep loneliness that gives rise to a hunger for intimacy, one that exists *before* the two people meet, and in the withdrawal. The first, a preparation for infatuation, teaches us that persons are inwardly disposed toward intimacy such that when they meet another who is also so disposed, the encounter promotes an emptying of those inner seeds that carry with them the potential for love: tenderness, acceptance, understanding, respect, and simplicity. These are the interior seeds of love that *seem* to come to fruition in the infatuated encounter. But in the final phase of infatuation, the withdrawal, the lovers discover that the seeds of love cannot be forced to fruition through the mere exercise of will. It is this final phase that "sends us out in darkness," that promotes an awareness of the poverty of immediate reality and enables us to be lonely. To appreciate the transformative power of these two phases, we have to be willing to dwell with the darkness of loneliness. We have to believe that death is not an end but a liberation, a barrenness in service of regeneration.

THE FINAL PHASE:
MORTIFICATION AND LIBERATION

In the final phase of infatuation, one lover, and perhaps both, begins to feel the pressure of the idealization of love. The reality of the other's limits or negative characteristics can no longer be easily contained by illusion. The charm of the mythopoetic fantasy begins to lose its seductive grasp. The tiniest rent or tear begins to show in the fabric of illusion. Both lovers begin to slowly awaken from the dream world of romance.

The awakening requires caution. To stand on the side of illusion is to be without hope, to see only destruction. To stand on the side of reality is to move out of a tense and feeble dream world into a world of solidity and strength, but that movement requires travel through the barren land of loneliness.

Infatuated people see no hope in this final phase. For them, the awakening is rather subtle and insidious. Every now and then, this or that negative characteristic asserts itself in a way that will not permit itself to be glamorized. The parties have a lovers' quarrel, and because their love is now threatened, they must hasten to "patch things up." Previously, they had only to face the pressure of a society from which they had secluded themselves. Now their relationship is assaulted by an internal pressure: honesty! In the quarrel, someone has spoken the unspeakable. The wart is seen as a wart, not as a beauty mark! Once the taboo about speaking reality is broken, infatuated persons begin to feel that perhaps their intimacy was founded on illusion, that perhaps they are not really loved at all. They begin to question. They begin to wonder if they are really loved for themselves or if they are serving some need in the other. Are they really seen by their lovers? Or are they an invention of the loved ones' imaginations? It begins not to matter so much that a very real, genuine part of who they are is accepted, understood, and affirmed. What matters is that distortion is at work. A very real part of what they are is found to be missing in the relationship, and they do not like it! As yet, they may be unable to see *their* own distortion of their loved ones. But they do begin to see how they have been victimized by romantic illusion with its promise of perfection. The awareness of life's harshness, of the poverty of immediate reality, has begun. Still, they are quick to forgive. But the seeds of distrust are sown, and in their immaturity they find themselves becoming a bit vigilant toward the other. Now they are bent on keeping their lovers honest, and, with the assertion of this value, illusion stands little hope of recapturing the previous claim it made upon their perception. They are less and less bent on false myth and more and more bent on reality.

In the final phase, respect, the foundation on which interpersonal honesty rests, emerges as a lived possibility. But before respect can be actualized in loving encounter, infatuated lovers will be struck down by reality. The illusion they have been living will be more and more jostled out of their relationship. They will begin to see that they are entitled to their limits and imperfections. The salvation illusion will be seen as an impertinent gate-crasher. Its insolent intrusion will not be tolerated, not through the exercise of will but simply because the stronger force of reality impinges itself on the weaker force of fantasy. The myth spun by their romantic imagination will be forced out of the relationship, and a reality whose power is experienced as beyond the will of the participants will quietly, gently, but forcefully call the lovers to task. But in its wake, the retreating illusion will leave shame and doubt.

In the final phase, the lovers will see that the very erotic nature of their feelings of unity with the beloved has created a circumstance of loneliness. But this loneliness will carry with it the possibility of a deeper kinship with their fellow man, a kinship in which urgency will be transformed into freedom and choice. In this final phase, they will have moved from twilight with its "rich" illusion to daylight with its poverty, but they will feel a curious sense of relief, of the kind that comes when pressure is removed. The lovers will feel the "deep loneliness." Yet they will feel free of their erotic urgency. Loneliness is the remedy of infatuation. Nostalgic longing had concealed the loneliness. Yet the loneliness had persisted, and in the end it became the agent of transformation. It converts love's urgent longing into affectivity, that tender, respectful witness that husbands intimate knowing and respectful love. The next chapter addresses this final phase of infatuation and examines how this special kind of loneliness, this "urgent longing," promotes the respectful intimacy of intimate knowing, what Dunne teaches us is a "longing that seeks communion with God."[13]

---

13. Dunne, p. 58.

V

THE ALLOWING SELF
AND INTIMATE KNOWING

One dark night
Fired by love's urgent longings
—Ah, the sheer grace!—
I went out unseen
My house being now all stilled.

St. John of the Cross
"The Dark Night"

In telling the story of human intimacy, we have spoken of loneliness and searching, urgency and illusion, enthusiasm and disappointment; these sentiments constitute love's disturbing darkness. But St. John's poem speaks of peace and stillness.

Is there a practical way to tell infatuated people that darkness and peace stem from the same root? Obviously, it would be a mistake to tell disappointed lovers that peace, or inner stillness, will come if only they are patient. Disappointed people tend to be cynical and resentful. They do not want to listen to stories that tell of patience and peace. Perhaps repressive people have the right idea: when the erotic feelings of infatuated love begin to bud, we should prune them quickly and severely. Certainly, we are tempted to do so when people in the final throes of infatuation, having suffered through love's enthusiam, must now

97

witness love's disappointment with all its attendant shame, guilt, and resentment.

LOVE'S ENTHUSIASM: INFATUATION'S ACTIVE NIGHT

At first the urgent enthusiasm of infatuated people for each other encircled them in fantasy, making them inaccessible. In their later disappointment, they hide either in their rooms or in their sour dispositions. In any event, they are again inaccessible, indeed, even more remote than they were before. Communication assumes considerable importance in such situations. Lovers fired with enthusiasm are difficult enough to manage, but lovers disillusioned with love are a severe trial even for those whose patience might make them worthy of beatification.

It is hard not to be irritated with disappointed lovers. They seem intent on making us lose our patience. We might even be tempted to speculate that they are engaged in a very deliberate and malevolent attempt to reveal our personal limitations. This speculation is not as idle as we might imagine. Their story is one of imperfection, limits, and poverty; so it is not surprising that that story is the only one they are willing or able to hear.

But before we consider shifting from husbanding to repression, we should recall the flow of events in the phenomenon of infatuation. Persons first experience a feeling of utter aloneness; they meet someone who appears as if in a dream; they are touched in understanding and acceptance; they are fired with love's enthusiasm, but the experience is accompanied by pressure and tension; they move in and out of the dream; then they suffer a period of disappointment, in which they are disillusioned, embarrassed, ashamed, guilty, and wracked with self-doubt. Under such circumstances, who could maintain a sense of humor? A sour disposition is a reasonable response to such feelings. Still, disappointed people are a trial because it is difficult to witness to their resentment.

When enthused, the lovers are often a delight. There are times when they clearly transcend the pressure and struggle of their relationship. At such moments, they seem to inspire everyone in their company. But when they are disappointed, they seem to turn against everyone, including themselves.

To understand infatuated persons, we must remember that love's period of enthusiasm is also a dark night. When we look at the smiling faces of lovers, it is difficult to believe this statement. But infatuation begins with a feeling of darkness, of utter aloneness. Thus love's enthusiasm flows from a moment of poverty. The poverty of aloneness fosters in infatuated persons a feeling of their own insignificance. They question their worth; they feel unacceptable. They lack understanding. They believe that they are unknown and that no one cares. It is in the midst of such feelings that they stumble onto someone whose very presence offers promise of relief. Touched by an understanding, accepting person while in the throes of utter aloneness, they respond in enthusiasm. It is the natural response of those who fear they are condemned to be alone and will never be chosen. Having been touched, now feeling they can be known, they seek insurance; they experience love's urgency. Their enthusiasm is the song of celebration that flows from hunger satisfied. However, the painful memory of loneliness does not disappear. Indeed, it is the springboard of their enthusiasm. They remember all too clearly how they felt before they were touched by love, and they have no desire to return to that state.

Love's enthusiasm springs from the hunger of fear. It is an active search, an urgency to maintain the status quo, a fear that loneliness will return. It is hard to believe that these lovers never leave behind the poverty that prompted their infatuation. Yet if we look into the face of someone enthused by love, we see self-consciousness. We see a struggle to maintain happiness. We see traces of the first night in the search for love, a night St. John's theology refers to as an "active night of the senses," accented by urgency and illusion.

SHAME, GUILT, AND ISOLATION: LOVE'S PASSIVE NIGHT

While struggling to maintain the illusion of happiness, infatuated people must put themselves beyond reach of reality's harsh touch. Lovers are thus irrational, beyond reason. They are beyond the reach of people who in their wisdom comprehend both the situation and the implications of the lovers' behavior. The self-conscious face of an infatuated person is that of someone torn between two realities, unable to choose between either. Infatuated persons are quite literally "out of their minds." They reason with their hearts, or, as Pascal said: "The heart has its reasons that reason does not know."[1] Their minds are not yet prepared to accept the rational wisdom of others.

Adolescents or young novices who feel they are in love with older teachers or professed are not yet able to comprehend either their feelings or their situation; they are

---

1. Quoted in John Dunne, *Reasons of the Heart* (New York: Macmillan, 1978), p. xii.

beyond the insightful reasoning of others; they are beyond reach of practical reality. They have been fired by love's urgent longing, and they are spontaneously, unreflectively moved to seek love actively; this goal is their overpowering inclination, their urgent desire. They believe in their hearts that they are responding to the call of love, and they can hear no other call. Those outside the circle of love reason with the intellect, from the perspective of insight already developed and tested by experience. However, such people would do well to remember John Dunne's lesson that one is first touched by the heart's reason and then by the mind's reason.[2] One is *ap*prehended by reality before one *com*prehends that reality. Infatuated people are neither ready nor able to hear the comprehending reason of insight others have to offer, regardless of its wisdom. First their yearning for love's intimacy will have to become the darkness of deep longing. First the urgent hunger for love must deepen in anguish; the grasping urgency of desire must loosen and die before the stillness of insight can occur. The agitation, the self-consciousness, the darkness promoted by love's urgent longing with its attendant suffering must be experienced before the allowing self of insight can emerge. Those beyond the lovers' circle cannot use their own insight to chase away illusion. Before the heart's reason can yield to the mind's reason, urgency has to diminish. Infatuated persons have to undergo what Charles Maes calls "the death of desire."[3]

Indeed, when we look into the self-conscious face of someone in love, we see a struggle with desire. We see

---

2. Ibid.

3. Charles Maes, unpublished lecture on psychoanalysis, Duquesne University, Pittsburgh, Pennsylvania, March 10, 1976.

desire and the fear of being alone. When we look at that same face in the throes of disappointed love, we see the poverty it has been struggling so hard to hide. We see the face of loneliness. Persons whose faces are so easily read react with embarrassment and resentment. They consider it unfitting to be seen in their poverty, and they are right. We must be content with only an occasional glance at such faces.

Recall what has already been said about mythopoeisis and the moment when the web of illusion begins to tear. At that moment each lover discovers that neither has accepted the other's limits and imperfections, that each has attempted to force the reality of the other to conform to his own image of perfection. It is at this point that insight is possible. It is a curious irony that the agent of that insight is a negative experience. When the lovers mutually discover their attempts to change each other, they react with a sense of shame that eventually deepens and becomes guilt. When we see the disappointed faces of those suffering the death of desire, we are looking at persons who have become aware of their nakedness.

What is this shame? What is this nakedness? It is an awareness of self. These persons are reacting to their vision of their own behavior. They recognize that they have violated a fundamental principle of human intimacy. They have been neither open nor accepting. Illusion has been stripped away, and shame forces them to peer into their hearts. They are forced to look at themselves. They are made to be truly and profoundly conscious of self with all its imperfection.

What they see is the behavior of one who has tried to force acceptance to occur without the tolerant, receptive openness that cultivates the growth of real understanding. Their shame is a vision of the heart. It is that wisdom those outside the circle of love call "common sense."[4] Without the distraction of illusion, they see that they have tried to put being accepted and being understood *before* acceptance and understanding, and they are ashamed.

Their shame grasps a fundamental truth about the life of intimacy. Their shame is not merely the embarrassment of being found out; it is the awareness of a deeply rooted belief in the autonomy and freedom of human existence. Curiously, *scham,* the German root of the English word "shame," means kinship, relationship. Infatuated people are ashamed because they feel negative about something that is essential, fundamental, and positive for human living, something that emerges from a deep respect and tolerance of others. That something is the recognition that as we move toward others we must do so in a manner that guarantees their integrity, their freedom to be who and what they are, with all their gifts and flaws.

The guilt that attends the final phase of infatuation creates a particularly difficult problem for anyone counseling infatuated persons, especially if they have been genitally involved. On the deeper spirit level, the shame and guilt have nothing to do with matters of morality. Rather, this guilt is an existential instruction. It reflects the wisdom that they have actively sought to make intimacy happen without the self-surrender, the self-emptying, the letting go in faith that allows us human beings to get detached from

---

4. Alfred Schutz, *Collected Papers* (The Hague: Martinus Nijhoff, 1970). The concept of common sense as "sentience" or sensing-knowing is developed throughout the collected works, particularly in his essays on common sense.

our urgent need for acceptance. This guilt reflects the wisdom that we humans can be intimate only when we are tolerant and respectfully guarantee the freedom of others, particularly the freedom to reject our overtures of love and affection. Infatuated persons now understand they were so caught up in their urgency to be loved that they were estranged from intimacy, distracted by the *ignis fatuus* of need.

In this final phase of infatuation, the self-conscious face is gone, displaced by the face of disappointment. We no longer see a face torn between the poverty of loneliness and the illusion of infatuation. We see only disappointment.

The face of disappointment has its own story to tell, but like the self-conscious face, it fears being alone. Yet it is not a face torn in two. It is a face in dialogue with illusion and loneliness. Whereas before it looked into the mirror of illusion and believed it saw perfection, now it sees through the illusion to life's harshness, and this perception has a force that cannot be denied. To catch such a glimpse of reality requires an intimate moment, a moment that needs privacy. Shame and guilt provide the impetus to be alone.

Somewhere deep within, infatuated persons realize the profound vision they have been privileged to see, and they are embarrassed that persons as insignificant as they have been granted such a gift. But their lesson is not yet complete, for they are still unable to look others in the eye. So they remain alone and detached, even in the presence of others.

Once the web of illusion is torn, it is too feeble to be mended. Attempts to restore the happy face of illusion and to hide the fear of being alone only result in feelings of embarrassment with its attendant shame and guilt. Shame comes as a painful reminder, and guilt offers a powerful instruction; together these feelings become the healing voice of integrity, a voice that requires a retreat into solitude in order to be heard. The intimate vision infatuated persons have seen and the realization of what they have done promote the embarrassed look that reveals their attempt to conceal being imperfect.

Infatuation is love's novitiate. At this point in their lives, infatuated people have not yet attained the strength to accommodate real solitude. Indeed, for them the being alone that is essential for solitude would be an overwhelming experience. To the novice at love, solitude has no experiential value. Yet the infatuation experience carries within itself a means of accommodating this deficiency. Infatuated persons need to be alone, and the embarrassment of their failure in integrity forces the issue. Their brokenhearted pride simply will not tolerate the presence of others!

In their embarrassment, infatuated persons are forced to be alone, although their sour disposition is an attempt to seduce others into paying attention to them. Nonetheless, isolation permeates their existence in this "second night" of infatuation, more passive than the active night of enthusiasm, but during which they become even more difficult to live with. In their embarrassed isolation, they are undergoing a transformation to an other-centered attitude. Eventually, their tolerance of imperfection, in both themselves and others, will have deepened to the point that they are able to abandon isolation, look others in the eye, and allow themselves to be seen with all their flaws, limits, and imperfections.

CONCLUSION: THE LESSON
OF LOVE'S DARKNESS

The resolution of infatuation's second night, the "dark night" of disappointment, brings the episode of infatuation full circle. Infatuated persons begin their journey with an experience of utter aloneness, and they conclude it with an embarrassed isolation. At the beginning and end they are alone, but their ending loneliness is of a different sort. They feel this loneliness as somehow different. They feel a bit more solid, a bit more sure of who and what they are. During their painful excursion into love, they have confronted *kenosis*. The thoughts that flow from their embarrassed state are long thoughts. They can linger in their loneliness, for they have been liberated from their prison of urgency through the redemptive mystery of suffering.

Liberated from urgency, the longing and loneliness are somehow a bit more acceptable. The sense of being alone lacks the awkwardness it has at the height of the infatuated state. Now, in their isolation, infatuated persons discover that it is impossible to stand before others and hide human imperfection. In their isolation, they can come home to themselves.

While accepting responsibility for violating the integrity of their perceptions, they experience an intimacy with self; they feel an inner harmony, a healing of desire and action that enables them to begin to stand alone. The urgent desire for acceptance and the fear of rejection no longer dominate their attention. A concern for others and for self emerges. In speaking of the spiritual journey, John Dunne characterizes this state as one of "happy aloneness" in which self-conscious introspection becomes contemplation.[5] Quoting Kafka, Dunne describes contemplation as "a standpoint where one is neither before others nor before oneself but where everything is before one, where one is like someone 'gazing in front of him, but lost in thought and is oblivious of everything but free and untroubled, as if he were alone with nobody to observe him.' It is not a lack of self-consciousness as one had originally feared. Rather, one has to pass through and beyond the standpoint of self-consciousness to reach it. One has to go from a consciousness of oneself to a willingness to be oneself."[6] In their isolation, infatuated persons dwell on their pain. They meditate on the desire to be touched on the personal level. They come to the realization that in the introspective life they discovered only their pervasive imperfection. They know they were self-absorbed and self-conscious. They are at the edge of passing into the contemplative life.

Like Alice in Lewis Carroll's *Through The Looking Glass,* infatuated persons must pass through the mirror of their own reflection in order to see from the perspective of others, in order to imagine what it is like in the others' world. They can then return home with their world enlarged, enriched, and deepened. In their embarrassed isolation, they are like Alice after her first excursion into Wonderland.[7] They have suffered through the distorted, frightening, lonely journey of their own fantasy land. They

---

5. Dunne, p. 43.

6. Ibid.

7. Lewis Carroll's classic work is actually the story of two journeys, the first found in *Alice in Wonderland,* the second in *Through the Looking Glass.*

have returned from the rabbit hole of infatuation. They have passed through an awkward, self-conscious awareness of self. They have yet to pass into the world of others, but they have surmounted the first obstacle.

In the embarrassed isolation of infatuation's final phase, infatuated people are confronted with the choice of whether to be themselves. Dunne suggests that when one assents to be one's self, "one steps into the mirror image of oneself that has been blocking one's view and one becomes able to see the universe, to commune with all things."[8] In a word, one becomes a contemplative.

In the interpersonal life, infatuated persons have only just begun their journey to contemplation. In their embarrassed isolation, their urgent need to be affirmed begins to die. With this "death of desire" they are left with only nostalgia, a loneliness that is a longing for communion. With the death of urgency, they are at the brink of a new discovery: they must suspend their self-centered needs in order to make room for a loving other. In meditating on their long thoughts, they learn that intimate acceptance occurs when its search is suspended. With this meditation comes the most powerful wisdom of all: love is inaccessible when pursued.

Dunne says that "God is wild"; St. John the Apostle says that "God is Love." In the embarrassed isolation of infatuation, the spiritual and human journeys intersect. Infatuated people discover that love is wild. It is not able to be grasped by urgency. In embarrassed isolation, shame and guilt put infatuated people in touch with the insights

---

8. Dunne, p. 43.

that solitude does not promote escape from but unity with others,[9] that communion and solitude are conjoined.[10]

Eventually, the awkward self-consciousness dissipates. The sour disposition sweetens a little, and infatuated persons are able to return to the world. But they are changed, for now they have learned that real intimacy is possible only when we are able to say to each other: we are alone together, you and I, and we cannot make each other unalone.[11] For those living with infatuated people, a final caution is in order. We must not expect such an utterance to be proclaimed with pomp and ceremony. It will not be delivered with any booming oratory. The best one can hope for is a barely audible squeak. But after the ecstasy and agony of infatuation, this squeak will be as awesome as the sound of the Seventh Trumpet (Apoc. 11:15-19)!

---

9. Thomas Merton, *New Seeds of Contemplation* (Gethsemani, KY: New Directions Press, 1972), pp. 52-61.

10. Henry Bugbee, "Loneliness, Solitude, and the Twofold Way in Which Concern Seems To Be Claimed," *Humanitas* 15 (1974): pp. 313-28.

11. John Dunne, *Time and Myth* (Notre Dame, IN: Notre Dame University Press, 1973), pp. 85-117.

APPENDIX A

THE DARK NIGHT

STANZAS OF THE SOUL

1. One dark night,
   Fired with love's urgent longings
   —Ah, the sheer grace!—
   I went out unseen,
   My house being now all stilled;

2. In darkness, and secure,
   By the secret ladder, disguised,
   —Ah, the sheer grace!—
   In darkness and concealment,
   My house being now all stilled;

3. On that glad night,
   In secret, for no one saw me,
   Nor did I look at anything,
   With no other light or guide
   Than the one that burned in my heart;

4. This guided me
   More surely than the light of noon
   To where He waited for me
   —Him I knew so well—
   In a place where no one else appeared.

5. O guiding night!
   O night more lovely than the dawn!
   O night that has united
   The Lover with His beloved,
   Transforming the beloved in her Lover.

6. Upon my flowering breast
   Which I kept wholly for Him alone,
   There He lay sleeping,
   And I caressing Him
   There in a breeze from the fanning cedars.

7. When the breeze blew from the turret
   Parting His hair,
   He wounded my neck
   With His gentle hand,
   Suspending all my senses.

8. I abandoned and forgot myself,
   Laying my face on my Beloved;
   All things ceased: I went out from myself,
   Leaving my cares
   Forgotten among the lilies.*

*The Collected Works of St. John of the Cross, trans. Kieran Kavanaugh and Otilio Rodriguez (Washington, DC: Institute of Carmelite Studies Publications, 1973), pp. 295-96.

APPENDIX B

THE SPIRITUAL CANTICLE

STANZAS BETWEEN THE SOUL
AND THE BRIDEGROOM

Bride

1. Where have You hidden,
Beloved, and left me moaning?
You fled like the stag
After wounding me;
I went out calling You, and You were gone.

2. Shepherds, you that go
Up through the sheepfolds to the hill,
If by chance you see
Him I love most,
Tell Him that I sicken, suffer, and die.

3. Seeking my love
I will head for the mountains and for watersides,
I will not gather flowers,
Nor fear wild beasts;
I will go beyond strong men and frontiers.

4. O woods and thickets
Planted by the hand of my Beloved!
O green meadow,
Coated, bright, with flowers,
Tell me, has He passed by you?

5. Pouring out a thousand graces,
He passed these groves in haste;
And having looked at them,
With His image alone,
Clothed them in beauty.

6.   Ah, who has the power to heal me?
Now wholly surrender Yourself!
Do not send me
Any more messengers,
They cannot tell me what I must hear.

7.   All who are free
Tell me a thousand graceful things of You;
All wound me more
And leave me dying
Of, ah, I-don't-know-what behind their
    stammering.

8.   How do you endure
O life, not living where you live?
And being brought near death
By the arrows you receive
From that which you conceive of your Beloved.

9.   Why, since You wounded
This heart, don't You heal it?
And why since You stole it from me,
Do You leave it so,
And fail to carry off what You have stolen?

10. Extinguish these miseries,
Since no one else can stamp them out;
And may my eyes behold You,
Because You are their light,
And I would open them to You alone.

11. Reveal Your presence,
And may the vision of Your beauty be my death;
For the sickness of love
Is not cured
Except by Your very presence and image.

12. O spring like crystal!
If only, on your silvered-over face,
You would suddenly form
The eyes I have desired,
Which I bear sketched deep within my heart.

Bridegroom
13. Withdraw them, Beloved,
I am taking flight!
  Return, dove,
The wounded stag
Is in sight on the hill,
Cooled by the breeze of your flight.

Bride
14. My Beloved is the mountains,
And lonely wooded valleys,
Strange islands,
And resounding rivers,
The whistling of love-stirring breezes,

15. The tranquil night
At the time of the rising dawn,
Silent music,
Sounding solitude,
The supper that refreshes, and deepens love.

16. Catch us the foxes,
For our vineyard is now in flower,
While we fashion a cone of roses
Intricate as the pine's;
And let no one appear on the hill.

17. Be still, deadening north wind;
South wind come, you that waken love,
Breathe through my garden,
Let its fragrance flow,
And the Beloved will feed amid the flowers.

18. You girls of Judea,
While among flowers and roses
The amber spreads its perfume,
Stay away, there on the outskirts:
Do not so much as seek to touch our
    thresholds.

19. Hide Yourself, my Love;
Turn Your face toward the mountains,
And do not speak;
But look at those companions
Going with her through strange islands.

Bridegroom

20. Swift-winged birds,
Lions, stags, and leaping roes,
Mountains, lowlands, and river banks,
Waters, winds, and ardors,
Watching fears of night:

21. By the pleasant lyres
And the siren's song, I conjure you
To cease your anger
And to touch the wall,
That the bride may sleep in deeper peace.

22. The bride has entered
The sweet garden of her desire,
And she rests in delight,
Laying her neck
On the gentle arms of her Beloved.

23. Beneath the apple tree:
There I took you for My own,
There I offered you My hand,
And restored you,
Where your mother was corrupted.

Bride

24. Our bed is in flower,
Bound round with linking dens of lions,
Hung with purple,
Built up in peace,
And crowned with a thousand shields of gold.

25. Following Your footprints
Maidens run along the way;
The touch of a spark,
The spiced wine,
Cause flowings in them from the balsam of God.

26. In the inner wine cellar
I drank of my Beloved, and, when I went abroad
Through all this valley
I no longer knew anything,
And lost the herd which I was following.

27. There He gave me His breast;
There He taught me a sweet and living knowledge;
And I gave myself to Him,
Keeping nothing back;
There I promised to be His bride.

28. Now I occupy my soul
And all my energy in His service;
I no longer tend the herd,
Nor have I any other work
Now that my every act is love.

29. If, then, I am no longer
Seen or found on the common,
You will say that I am lost;
That, stricken by love,
I lost myself, and was found.

30. With flowers and emeralds
Chosen on cool mornings
We shall weave garlands
Flowering in Your love,
And bound with one hair of mine.

31. You considered
That one hair fluttering at my neck;
You gazed at it upon my neck
And it captivated You;
And one of my eyes wounded You.

32. When You looked at me
Your eyes imprinted Your grace in me;
For this You loved me ardently;
And thus my eyes deserved
To adore what they beheld in You.

33. Do not despise me;
For if, before, You found me dark,
Now truly You can look at me
Since You have looked
And left in me grace and beauty.

Bridegroom
34. The small white dove
Has returned to the ark with an olive branch;
And now the turtledove
Has found its longed-for mate
By the green river banks.

35. She lived in solitude,
And now in solitude has built her nest;
And in solitude He guides her,
He alone, Who also bears
In solitude the wound of love.

Bride

36. Let us rejoice, Beloved,
And let us go forth to behold ourselves in Your beauty,
To the mountain and to the hill,
To where the pure water flows,
And further, deep into the thicket.

37. And then we will go on
To the high caverns in the rock
Which are so well concealed;
There we shall enter
And taste the fresh juice of the pomegranates.

38. There You will show me
What my soul has been seeking,
And then You will give me,
You, my Life, will give me there
What You gave me on that other day:

39. The breathing of the air,
The song of the sweet nightingale,
The grove and its living beauty
In the serene night,
With a flame that is consuming and painless.

40. No one looked at her,
Nor did Aminadab appear;
The siege was still;
And the cavalry,
At the sight of the waters, descended.*

The Collected Works of St. John of the Cross, trans. Kieran Kavanaugh and Otilio Rodriguez (Washington, DC: Institute of Carmelite Studies, 1973), pp. 410-15.